THE AUSTRALIAN BANANA RECIPE BOOK

Photographs by David Hammond

First published 1994 by Southern Holdings Pty Ltd
P.O. Box 6, Huonville 7109, Australia.
© Copyright 1994 by Southern Holdings Pty Ltd
ACN 009550841

ISBN 094 9089 33 8

* * * * *

**This book is available from the publishers, Southern Holdings Pty Ltd
P.O. Huonville 7109, for $6.95 plus $1.60 P & P.
or Phone/Fax (002) 664112**

Contents

About Bananas...

Bananas do not set seed, and have been grown from suckers for hundreds of years. A herbaceous plant from South East Asia, the banana grows best in a frost free, hot wet climate. Each plant has one fruiting stem. It grows one crop of fruit and is cut down to ground level after harvest. Suckers grow around the fruiting stem, and one of these will become the fruiting stem the next year.

Each flowering stem produces one *bunch* of between 5 and 15 *hands* of fruit, weighing from 15 kg to 25kg. Each banana is called a *finger*. Plastic covers, open at top and bottom, are placed around each bunch of fruit to protect it from leaf rub, sunburn, birds and pests. Fruit is harvested at various stages of ripeness, depending on the market destination. On arrival it can be ripened by exposure to ethylene gas.

Bananas (Nature's Energy Bar) have a high food value and are easily digested; that is why they are often the first solid food given to young babies. Bananas contain plenty of protein, vitamins A, B & C, iron, magnesium, phosphorus, potassium and other minerals important for healthy development. They taste terrific and are used in baked dishes, pies, salads, desserts and fruit drinks.

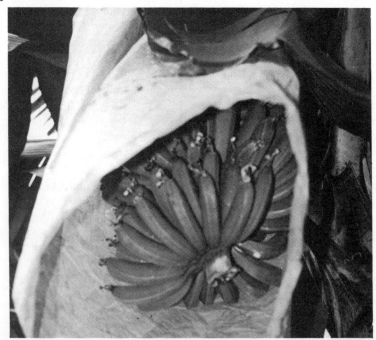

Savouries & Snacks

Scalloped Bananas

3 bananas, peeled
1/2 teaspoon salt
1 cup crushed cornflakes
1 egg, beaten
Little melted butter

Mix salt into egg. Slice bananas in three lengthwise then dip pieces in egg. Coat thickly with cornflakes then fry in butter until golden both sides. Serve hot with grilled meat, ham or chicken. Serves 4.

Banana & Bean Savoury

1 banana, peeled, sliced
1 medium onion, chopped finely
140g tin tomato paste
Hot toast
440g tin red kidney beans
2 rashers bacon
Salt & pepper to taste

Saute thin strips of bacon until slightly browned, then remove from pan. Saute onion in pan drippings until translucent; add tomato paste. Simmer only a few seconds then add bacon, beans, salt & pepper. Heat through then quickly mix banana through; serve on hot toast.

Curried Bananas

1 dessertspoon curry powder
3 large bananas, peeled, sliced
1 dessertspoon brown sugar
Little lemon juice
30g butter

Brush lemon juice over banana, then place in heated pan with butter; cook gently, sprinkling sugar & curry, until brown and glazed.

Bananas Baked in Cranberry Sauce

6 medium bananas, peeled
1 cup whole-cranberry sauce
Salt
2 tablespoons butter, melted

Place bananas in shallow baking dish, brush butter over, then sprinkle salt. Pour sauce over, bake in moderate oven 15 minutes or until tender. Serve warm or cool. Makes 6.

Banana Pizza

Dough

1-1/2 cups flour	Pinch salt
1/2 teaspoon sugar	1 egg, beaten
3 teaspoons compressed yeast	1/4 cup milk, warm
6 teaspoons butter	

Sift flour & salt into bowl, then add sugar. Dissolve crumbled yeast in milk, add egg. Stir yeast mixture into flour mixture until blended. Cream butter then work into dough. Let covered bowl stand 40 minutes or until dough has doubled. Press into 23cm pizza pan or pie plate.

Filling

125g ham, chopped	1/4 cup tomato paste
250g tomatoes, peeled, sliced	1 dessertspoon oil
1 small onion, chopped	1/2 teaspoon oregano
125g mozzarella cheese, grated	2 medium bananas

Heat oil in frying pan; cook onion & oregano 2 to 3 minutes. Place banana slices around outside edge of pizza pastry, with tomato slices across centre; spread tomato paste over then sprinkle fried onion, cheese, then ham. Bake in hot oven 425°C, 30 minutes. Serves 4.

Ham & Banana Rolls

4 slices lean ham	4 bananas, peeled
1 tablespoon evaporated milk	8 small onions, peeled
Boiling water, salted	1/2 cup grated cheese

Simmer onions 5 minutes in salted water, then drain. Place 1 banana on each ham slice, roll up then put in small greased ovenproof dish; add onions & milk; sprinkle cheese. Bake in hot oven 20 minutes to heat through. Serve with mustard sauce.

Mustard Sauce

1 dessertspoon dry mustard	45g butter
1/4 cup flour	Salt & pepper
1-1/2 cups milk	

Melt butter in pan, stir in flour & mustard; cook 1 minute, then remove from heat. Add milk gradually, stirring; bring to boil, stirring, reduce heat. Simmer, stirring, until smooth & thickened; add salt & pepper.

Curry Sauce

2 ripe bananas
1 small green apple
1 tablespoon coconut
2-1/2 cups boiling water
3 chicken stock cubes
1-1/2 tablespoons curry powder
2 tablespoons red currant jelly

2 medium onions
2 tomatoes
60g butter
1/3 cup flour
1-1/2 cups milk
Juice 1 lemon
2 tablespoons mango chutney

Dissolve stock cubes in boiling water. Heat butter in pan; fry peeled, finely chopped bananas, apple, onions & tomatoes until brown, stirring occasionally. Add flour, curry & coconut; cook 2 to 3 minutes, then add stock gradually, add milk then cook, stirring until boiling. Reduce heat then add chutney, cover, simmer 30 minutes, stirring occasionally.

Add lemon & red currant; simmer further 15 minutes. Strain through sieve, pushing as much fruit through as possible to make thick sauce. Use with meat, vegetables, chicken & fish.

Banana Crepes & Cheese Sauce

1 tablespoon vegetable oil
8 small bananas, peeled
2 cups Swiss cheese, grated
1 cup thick white sauce
Salt, pepper & cayenne
Few drops Angostura bitters

1-1/3 cups flour
3 eggs
1/2 cup cream
Little butter, melted
1/2 teaspoon salt
Milk

Combine flour, eggs, oil & 1/2 teaspoon salt with about 1-1/2 cups milk to make smooth batter. Chill 1 hour then add more milk to make batter consistency of slightly whipped thick cream. Cook batter 1 side only in small pan to make 8 crepes about 150mm across. Put banana on each, sprinkle bitters, seasonings, 3 tablespoons cheese & 1 tablespoon white sauce, then roll crepe around banana. Place in shallow baking dish, brush butter over. Bake in hot oven 15 minutes.

Stir remaining cream & cheese into white sauce; pour over crepes, then cook further 8 minutes or until bananas are tender, with sauce just beginning to brown. Makes 8.

Banana Sandwiches

* Spread bread with peanut butter then top with banana slices & crumbled crisp bacon. Cover with bread.

* Spread white bread with mayonnaise then top with banana slices. Cover with bread slices spread with currant jelly.

* Mix together 1 cup chopped raisins, 1 teaspoon salt, & mayonnaise to moisten. Spread 4 slices of bread with mixture, then top with banana slices. Cover with slices of buttered bread.

Banana & Ham Sandwiches

3/4 cup finely chopped cooked ham	1/4 cup minced celery
2 teaspoons prepared mustard	Onion powder to taste
1 medium banana, finely diced	8 thin slices white bread
Mayonnaise or softened butter	Tomato slices or watercress

Mix ham, celery, mustard & onion, add banana then mix lightly. Spread bread lightly with mayonnaise, then spread 4 slices with banana mixture; top with remaining bread. Cut each sandwich in 2 triangles; garnish with cress.

Curried Banana & Bacon Sandwiches

2 medium bananas, peeled, diced	8 slices bacon
1 teaspoon lemon juice	1/4 cup mayonnaise
1/4 teaspoon curry powder	8 slices bread, toasted

Cook bacon until crisp; drain, crumble. Mix mayonnaise, lemon juice & curry powder, add to bananas, mixing carefully. Fold in crumbled bacon, then spread on toast. Makes 4 sandwiches.

Banana Storage

Store bananas to ripen at room temperature, except for fully ripe fruit, which can be stored in the refrigerator to retard over-ripening. The pulp remains flavourful even if the peel darkens. Very low temperatures retard ripening and impair delicate flavour.

French Toast Sandwiches

8 slices firm white bread
2 medium bananas cut in 10mm slices
Crisp bacon (optional)
Syrup, jam, sugar & cinnamon,OR icing sugar

2 eggs
1/2 cup milk
1/4 teaspoon salt

Make 4 sandwiches filled with banana slices. Beat eggs slightly with milk & salt. Dip each sandwich in mixture then brown slowly both sides in greased pan. Serve with syrup & bacon if liked.

Fruity Frankfurters

3 bananas, peeled, halved lengthwise
6 frankfurters, halved lengthwise
2 apples, cored, quartered

1/3 cup melted butter
1 teaspoon lemon juice
2 tablespoons brown sugar

Place franks, skin side down, in greased shallow baking dish. Put banana half on each frankfurter, arrange apple quarters around edge of dish. Mix butter, sugar & lemon juice, then brush generously over all. Bake in moderate oven 15 minutes, or until apples are tender.

BANANA FACTS

Bananas can be used at varying degrees of ripeness.

Slightly green-tipped bananas are excellent to cook, bake, broil or saute. Cooking makes partially ripe bananas fully digestible, and brings out a delicious and different flavour.

All-yellow bananas are firm enough to cook and ripe enough to eat and to use as an ingredient in cakes, breads, etc.

Fully ripe bananas are flecked with brown. These are best for fruit cups, salads, desserts, beverages, eating from the hand, and as an ingredient in baking.

To keep bananas from darkening when sliced, sprinkle with a little lemon juice.

To score bananas when using slices for decorating, peel then run tines of fork lengthwise along banana.

9

Salads

Banana Celery Salad

Combine equal amounts of diagonal slices of banana with thin diagonal slices of celery. Season mayonnaise generously with lime juice & celery seed, then pour over bananas & celery. Good with cold meat or seafood.

Banana Waldorf Salad

1 large red apple, unpeeled	1/2 cup diced celery
1/4 cup mayonnaise	2 medium bananas
!/2 cup walnut pieces	Salad greens

Dice apple in bite-size pieces, then toss with celery & mayonnaise. Peel & slice bananas, mix lightly with apple mixture. Arrange salad greens on 4 to 6 serving plates, add salad, garnish with nuts.

Banana, Apple & Date Salad

2 medium bananas, peeled, sliced	2 tablespoons thick cream
1/2 cup stoned dates	Juice 1/2 lemon
2 tart unpeeled red apples, diced	Salad greens
Mayonnaise or salad dressing	

Mix dates & cream. Sprinkle lemon juice over bananas, then mix lightly with apples & dates. Moisten with mayonnaise; serve on salad greens. Serves 4 to 6.

Warm Tropical Salad

1 passion fruit OR 2 tablespoons tinned passion fruit pulp

2 small bananas, peeled, sliced	1 small papaya, peeled, sliced
1 small rock melon, peeled, sliced	2 tablespoons butter
1 tablespoon sugar	
1/4 cup apple juice OR Moselle	

Melt butter & sugar in frying pan, then stir in bananas & papaya; heat through for 2 minutes; remove to warm plate. Put passion fruit pulp & seed into bowl. Add juice or wine to pan; cook 2 minutes to reduce a little then stir in passion fruit. When hot, pour over bananas & papaya then serve.

Jellied Banana & Pineapple Salad

2 pkts lemon or lime flavoured gelatin
1 250g tin crushed pineapple
1 teaspoon curry powder
1 cup thinly sliced celery

3 bananas, peeled
2 tablespoons lemon juice
Watercress

Mix gelatin & curry powder in 2 cups boiling water; stir until dissolved. Drain syrup from pineapple into 500ml measuring cup, add lemon juice then fill cup with cold water. Stir into gelatin mixture, pour thin layer into 20cm square baking pan; chill until firm.

Slice 1 banana lengthwise in thirds, arrange to make a design in the pan, then bind with another thin layer of gelatin. Chill remaining gelatin mixture until thickened but not firm. Slice remaining bananas then add to mixture with celery & pineapple; spoon into pan, chill until firm. Unmold, decorate with watercress. Serves 8.

Banana French Dressing

Mash 1 ripe banana in small bowl. Gradually beat in 1/2 cup bottled creamy French dressing. Chill. Serve with fruit salads, coleslaw, chicken or turkey salad. Makes 3/4 cup.

Banana Mayonnaise

1 ripe banana, peeled, mashed
1 tablespoon fresh lime/lemon juice

1/2 cup mayonnaise
1 teaspoon prepared mustard

Put all ingredients in bowl, beat or blend until smooth; cover, chill. Keeps well 4 to 5 days. Good with fruit, cold meat or seafood. Makes 1 cup.

Banana Honey Dressing

2 ripe bananas, peeled, mashed
2 tablespoons lemon juice
1/2 teaspoon paprika
1 teaspoon salt

1/2 cup salad oil
1/4 cup cider vinegar
1 tablespoon honey

Put all ingredients in bowl, beat or blend until smooth; cover, chill. Beat well before serving with fruit or greens. Keeps well 4 to 5 days. Makes 1-1/2 cups

Fish

Fish with Bananas

4 medium bananas   750g to 1kg fish fillets
Little melted butter   Dried breadcrumbs

Sauce

2 onions, chopped   110g butter
1 cup white wine   1-1/2 tablespoons plain flour
1-1/2 cups boiling water   2 beef stock cubes
1 tablespoon french mustard   Pinch sugar
Salt & pepper

Dip fillets in butter then coat with breadcrumbs; chill for 30 minutes. Grill both sides until golden brown and cooked through. Peel bananas, cut lengthwise then pan fry in a little butter until golden brown. Serve with sauce. Serves 4 - 6.

Sauce

Dissolve stock cubes in boiling water. Heat wine in saucepan until reduced by half. Fry onions in butter until golden; add flour and stir over low heat until lightly browned. Add stock & wine, bring to boil while stirring. Reduce heat, simmer 20 minutes stirring occasionally. Season to taste; add mustard & sugar. Strain.

Baked Shrimps with Bananas

750g frozen, cleaned, peeled shrimps   Melted butter
6 medium bananas, peeled   Sweet & sour sauce
Hot cooked rice (1 cup before cooking)   Salt, pepper & paprika

Put shrimps in greased shallow baking dish; brush with butter, sprinkle with salt, pepper & paprika. Bake in moderate oven 15 minutes. Arrange bananas in dish with shrimps; brush with butter, sprinkle paprika over; bake 15 minutes longer. Mound cooked shrimps & rice on hot serving plate, surround with bananas; serve immediately with sauce. Serves 6.

Sweet & Sour Sauce

Drain 1 large tin pineapple pieces, reserve syrup. In saucepan mix 1/3 cup sugar & 2 tablespoons cornflour. Add 1/4 cup cider vinegar, 1 tablespoon soy sauce, 1/4 teaspoon ginger & reserved syrup. Cook, stirring, until clear & thickened, then add pineapple, simmer two minutes. Makes 2-1/2 cups.

Curried Prawns

2 large bananas, peeled, sliced	500g prawns, peeled
4 sticks celery, sliced	3 tomatoes cut in wedges
3 onions, peeled, sliced	1/2 cup white wine
1 tablespoon curry powder	Juice 1/2 lemon
1-1/2 cups boiling water	1/4 cup extra water
2 chicken stock cubes	1-1/4 cups coconut
1/2 teaspoon turmeric	6 peppercorns
2 tablespoons cooking oil	Salt
1 dessertspoon cornflour	1 bayleaf
Pinch cinnamon	Hot, cooked rice

Dissolve stock cubes in boiling water, then soak coconut in this stock 15 minutes. Drain, pressing coconut to expel liquid; reserve liquid. Heat oil in frying pan; fry onions until light brown, add bananas, celery & tomatoes. Cook 5 minutes then add curry powder, all seasonings, reserved liquid & wine. Simmer, covered, 45 minutes, then sieve, pressing vegetables through as much as possible. Add lemon juice. Blend cornflour with extra water then add to curry sauce. Bring to boil, stirring, then reduce heat; simmer 2 minutes. Add prawns, heat through; serve with hot rice. Serves 4.

Main Meals

Veal & Banana Treat

1 large banana, sliced
4 thin veal steaks
4 thin slices gruyere cheese
Salt & pepper to taste

Butter for cooking
1 large egg, beaten
Breadcrumbs

Pound steaks thin if necessary; lay out and sprinkle seasonings on each, then slices of cheese & banana. Fold steaks over; fasten with toothpicks, then roll in egg & breadcrumbs. Chill 30 minutes then cook in butter, turning periodically until cooked through. Serves 4.

Pot Roasted Lamb

1 small leg of lamb
1 teaspoon brown sugar
1 tablespoon worcestershire
1 dessertspoon vinegar
2 tabléspoons chutney
Tomato sauce

1 tablespoon flour
Salt & pepper
6 teaspoons butter
1 cup water
2 large bananas, peeled, chopped

Rub flour into surface of meat, then sprinkle salt & pepper. Heat butter in heavy saucepan and brown meat slowly on all sides. Remove meat, drain fat and return one tablespoonful, return meat then add all other ingredients. Bring to boil then reduce heat; simmer covered 2 hours or until tender. Turn & baste meat every 20 minutes. Serves 4 to 6.

Banana Meatloaf

1-1/2 cups mashed banana
1 tablesoon finely chopped onion
2 teaspoons worcestershire
2 cups soft breadcrumbs lightly packed

1kg minced beef
2 teaspoons salt
1/2 teaspoon pepper

Lightly mix all ingredients except banana, then add banana; mix lightly but thoroughly. Press into 23 X 12cm loaf tin; bake in moderate oven about 1 hour.
Serves 6 - 8.

Meatballs in Brown Sauce

750g minced hamburger
2 tablespoons tomato sauce
1 small banana, mashed
1 teaspoon dry mustard
1 onion, chopped finely

1/2 cup grated cheese
1 egg
Salt & pepper
Little butter

Combine all ingredients, mixing thoroughly in bowl. Form tablespoons of mixture into balls, with floured hands. Flatten slightly then fry in only enough butter to avoid sticking to pan; brown both sides. Place meatballs in sauce; bring to boil then reduce heat, cover and simmer 15 minutes or until cooked through.

Brown Sauce

1 chicken stock cube
1/4 cup butter, melted
Salt & pepper

1/3 cup flour
2 cups boiling water

Dissolve stock cube in water. Place butter in pan over heat; add flour, stirring until dark golden brown; remove from heat. Add stock gradually, mix well then return to heat. Bring to boil, season, remove from heat. Serves 4.

Lamb with Banana & Pineapple

1.25kg to 1.5kg lean breast of lamb
1/4 cup packed brown sugar
1/2 teaspoon dry mustard
440g tin pineapple pieces
2 medium bananas, chopped
Chopped parsley to sprinkle

1 large onion, chopped
3 cups water
Salt & pepper
1/4 cup soy sauce
1/4 cup vinegar

Trim excess fat from meat, then cut into riblets; place in large frying pan to brown, then drain fat. Add onion, water, salt & pepper; bring to boil. Cover then simmer 1 hour or until tender.

Drain pineapple, reserve syrup. In small saucepan combine syrup, sugar, soy sauce, vinegar & mustard; bring to boil, simmer 10 minutes.

Drain riblets then arrange in ovenproof dish; add bananas & pineapple pieces. Pour sauce over then bake uncovered in hot oven 15 minutes. Sprinkle parsley before serving. Serves 4.

Curried Chops & Bananas

1 kg neck chops
2 large onions, peeled, chopped
2 tablespoons flour
1-1/2 tablespoons curry powder
25mm green ginger, chopped finely
1 tablespoon sultanas
Little brown sugar & curry powder to sprinkle

2 cups water
2 chicken stock cubes
Rind 1 lemon, grated
1 teaspoon salt & pepper
1 stick celery, chopped
4 cups boiled rice

Mix together flour, curry powder, salt & pepper. Trim chops of gristle & fat then roll in curry mixture; fry in little oil or butter in large saucepan until brown. Add onions, cook until transparent, then pour off excess fat. Dissolve cubes in water and add to pan with ginger, celery and lemon rind. Simmer, covered 1 hour, then add sultanas; simmer 3/4 hour or until chops are tender. Serve on rice; top with curried bananas, garnish with lemon wedges & parsley.

Chicken Maryland

4 chicken breasts with wing on to the first joint
100g seasoned flour
40g butter
1 egg, beaten

1 cup breadcrumbs
200ml cooking oil
Little milk

Combine egg with milk. Roll chicken breasts in flour then egg mixture; coat with breadcrumbs. Heat butter & oil then saute chicken both sides until golden brown; drain excess oil then place chicken in casserole dish; bake in moderate oven 30 minutes or until cooked. Serve with fried banana & corn fritters.

Corn Fritters

100g plain flour
1 teaspoon baking powder
100g frozen/tinned corn kernels

50ml milk
1 egg, separated
Salt & pepper

Sift flour with baking powder, salt & pepper. Beat egg yolk with milk, add corn then mix thoroughly with flour mixture. Beat egg white until stiff then fold in. Fry dessertspoons of mixture until golden brown. Serves 4.

Fried Bananas

4 bananas
1 egg

50g breadcrumbs

Cut bananas in half lengthwise, dip in egg then roll in breadcrumbs. Fry in oil until golden brown both sides.

Baked Savoury Dish

500g sausage meat
3/4 cup soft breadcrumbs
2 tomatoes, peeled, sliced
2 tablespoons flour
1 teaspoon curry powder
1 egg, hardboiled, chopped
1 dessertspoon worcestershire
1/2 small onion, chopped
2 large bananas, peeled, sliced
1 large onion, chopped
1 apple, peeled, sliced
45g butter
Salt & pepper
Pinch dry herbs
1/2 teaspoon dry mustard
3/4 cup water
Chopped parsley

Melt 15g butter in pan, brown breadcrumbs, then add to meat. Add egg, 1/2 onion, herbs & curry powder; season to taste, mixing well. Place mixture in greased ovenproof dish, then arrange bananas, apple, onion & tomato over.

Melt remaining butter in pan, add flour, stirring until golden; add mustard, then remove from heat. Add water gradually, return to heat then bring to boil; cook, stirring, until smooth & thickened, add sauce & seasonings. Pour sauce over tomatoes in casserole. Cover, bake in moderate oven 1 hour then remove cover, bake further 15 minutes. Sprinkle parsley. Serves 4.

Spicy Beef & Veg on Rice

1 kg topside steak
1 red capsicum, sliced
1 green capsicum, sliced
1-3/4 cups boiling water
2 chicken stock cubes
1/4 cauliflower
Oil for frying
Salt
3 medium bananas, peeled, chopped
4 medium onions, peeled, chopped
1 dessertspoon soy sauce
50mm green ginger, chopped
2 teaspoons turmeric
1/2 teaspoon chilli powder
Hot boiled rice

Dissolve stock cubes in boiling water. Cut trimmed meat in small strips. Heat oil in large frying pan, then add meat; brown quickly. Add ginger & onions; when starting to brown reduce heat, add turmeric, chilli powder, salt, soy sauce, bananas & stock. Bring to boil then reduce heat, simmer covered until tender. Boil cauliflower 4 minutes in separate saucepan, drain, add with sliced peppers to meat mixture. Cook 5 minutes then serve with rice.

Steak & Potato Pie

500g topside steak, cut in 25mm cubes
1 large onion, peeled, sliced
2 bananas, peeled, sliced
440g tin cream of tomato soup
1/3 cup sultanas

30g butter
Pinch nutmeg
Salt & pepper
Parsley
1 tablespoon flour

Heat butter in saucepan then saute steak until brown; remove from pan. Add onion, fry until golden; stir in flour, soup & seasoning. Return meat to pan then add bananas & sultanas. Bring to boil, reduce heat then cover; simmer stirring occasionally 1 hour or until meat tender. Pour into potato case then cover with remaining potato; brush with milk. Bake in moderately hot oven 30 minutes. Sprinkle parsley. Serves 4.

Potato Case

1 kg potatoes, peeled, boiled
1/4 cup milk

1 cup grated cheese
1 egg, beaten

Mash potato then add cheese, milk & egg; beat until smooth; season to taste. Line deep 23cm greased pie plate with half mixture; use remainder to top pie.

Ham & Banana Grill

2 kg ready to eat ham steaks
8 small bananas, peeled
2 tablespoons honey
Shredded coconut

3 tablespoons melted butter
1 teaspoon dry mustard
Grated rind 1 orange
Salt

Put ham on foil lined baking pan; bake in slow oven 30 minutes or until heated through. Mix butter, mustard, honey & orange rind until smooth, then brush top & sides of ham with part of mixture; grill 5 minutes. Arrange bananas around ham, sprinkle salt & brush honey mixture over. Grill 3 minutes or until bananas are almost tender, then sprinkle bananas with coconut, grill further 1 to 2 minutes or until coconut is lightly browned. Serve ham in thin diagonal slices, surrounded with bananas.

Serves 8. Recipe can be halved

To Mash Bananas

Slice ripe bananas into bowl. Beat with fork, rotary beater or electric mixer until smooth & creamy. Or whirl in blender to make more liquid product. One medium banana makes 1/3 to 1/2 cup of mashed banana.

Banana country, near Innisfail, Far North Queensland

Banana & Meat Rolls

750g ground beef
3 bananas, halved crosswise
1 cup lightly packed grated cheddar cheese
Worcestershire
Pepper

Divide meat into 6 equal portions; flatten each to make rectangle 130 X 100mm. Put banana half on each, sprinkle sauce & pepper over, then divide cheese evenly on each. Dip hands in cold water; use small spatula or knife blade to roll up meat around banana. Arrange in shallow baking dish, sprinkle sauce over, then bake in moderate oven 30 minutes. If desired, cut 3 tomatoes in half crosswise, sprinkle basil, salt & pepper over, then bake with rolls.

Savoury Dishes

Bananas can be served in place of a vegetable or as an extra side dish to a main meal. In a sauce they smooth the texture and enrich the flavour.

Desserts

Banana Squares

3 medium bananas, peeled, sliced
1/2 cup sugar
1 tablespoon extra sugar
1/2 teaspoon cinnamon
1 teaspoon grated lemon rind
Melted butter to brush
1 cup S.R. flour, sifted
1/4 cup butter
1/2 teaspoon salt
1/3 cup milk
1 egg, beaten

Combine flour, salt & sugar in bowl; rub in butter. Add egg & milk, stirring until well blended. Spread dough evenly in greased 28 X 18cm lamington tin. Combine extra sugar, lemon rind & cinnamon, then sprinkle over dough. Arrange banana on top; brush melted butter. Bake in moderate oven 35 minutes or until golden. Cut in squares, serve as cake or as dessert with whipped cream or custard.

Bananas Flambe

4 bananas
4 tablespoons brandy or kirsch
1/4 cup butter
sugar to sprinkle

Cut peeled bananas in half lengthwise, then cook in heated butter a few minutes. Add liqueur; when heated, set alight. Serve with ice cream or cream. Serves 4.

Banana Chiffon Cake

2 medium bananas, peeled, mashed
1-1/2 teaspoons baking powder
Grated rind, 1 lemon
1 teaspoon lemon juice
1/4 cup oil
Pinch cream of tartar

2 egg yolks
3/4 cup sugar
1-1/8 cups flour
Pinch salt
4 egg whites
Whipped cream

Sift flour, baking powder, sugar & salt in large basin of mixer, make well in centre then add oil, egg yolks, banana, rind & juice, then beat low speed about 4 minutes or until smooth. Beat egg whites with cream of tartar until peaking, then fold lightly into flour mixture without beating. Pour into greased 20cm baba tin; bake in moderately hot oven 55 to 60 minutes; cake should feel springy when pressed lightly with fingers.

When cooked, invert cake tin quickly then suspend until quite cold. Then shake tin to remove cake, split into 2 or 3 layers, fill with whipped cream & dust with icing sugar.

Fruit Salad Ice

1 banana, peeled, mashed
1/2 cup crushed pineapple, drained
1 cup sugar
1 cup water

Juice 1 lemon
Juice 1 orange
1 egg

Beat egg well, blend in lemon & orange juice, banana, pineapple, sugar & water. Freeze in freezer trays to make ice blocks, or icy poles. After freezing, flake lightly, then pile in chilled glass for delicious fresh flavour.

Caramel Bananas

4 large bananas, peeled, sliced
1 cup brown sugar
Thin pancakes

1/4 cup butter
1/4 cup cream

Heat butter in heavy frying pan; cook sugar, stirring periodically, until it dissolves and bubbles. Add bananas, cook until tender, then stir in cream. Pour over pancakes, serve with whipped cream or ice cream. Serves 4.

Banana Whip

1 cup undiluted evaporated milk   3 bananas, sliced
1 pkt pineapple, lemon *or* orange jelly crystals   1 cup boiling water
Pulp of 3 passion fruit

Chill milk overnight. Dissolve jelly crystals in water, allow to cool but not set. Whip chilled evaporated milk in chilled bowl until thick, then gradually beat in jelly mixture. Fold in bananas & passion fruit then spoon into serving dishes or one large mould; refrigerate until set. Serve with whipped cream or ice cream. Serves 4 - 6.

Baked Caramel Bananas

6 large bananas   Little flour
1/2 cup brown sugar   1/4 cup butter
1 tablespoon rum or sweet sherry

Cut peeled bananas in half lengthwise, then roll lightly in flour. Add rum to melted butter, remove from heat; pour half into base of greased ovenproof dish. Sprinkle half brown sugar, then put layer of banana over butter & sugar. Sprinkle remaining sugar, pour rest of butter mixture; cover then bake in moderately hot oven 15 to 20 minutes or until bananas are cooked but still firm. Serve hot with whipped cream or ice cream. Serves 6.

Apple & Banana Shortcake

2 apples, peeled, grated coarsely   1 large banana, sliced
Grated rind & juice 1/2 lemon   1/2 cup butter
Pulp 1 passionfruit   1 cup S.R. flour
1 cup castor sugar   1 cup plain flour
2 tablesoons extra castor sugar   1 egg, beaten
1/4 teaspoon salt

Cream butter & sugar lightly, add egg, beating well; mix in sifted flours & salt. Divide in two; roll each piece into ball; flatten into round, then place one round in 20cm greased sandwich tin. Cover with apple, banana & passionfruit. Sprinkle with lemon rind, juice & 1 tablespoon extra sugar; cover with second dough round, pressing sides well. Brush water over, sprinkle remaining extra sugar evenly, then bake in moderate oven 35 to 40 minutes.

Banana Pancakes

3 or 4 bananas, peeled
2 teaspoons baking powder
Oil or butter for frying
2-1/2 cups milk

2 cups flour
1/2 teaspoon salt
1 egg, beaten

Sift dry ingredients into bowl, add egg & enough milk to make fairly thin batter. Heat oil in pan; using 1/4 cup batter for each, fry pancakes until golden brown both sides; keep hot. Cut bananas lengthwise in quarters, then fill each pancake with banana; roll up, pour hot mocha sauce over.

Mocha Sauce

1-1/2 cups strong coffee
2 dessertspoons cornflour
2 dessertspoons butter

1 cup sugar
1 dessertspoon cocoa

Combine all ingredients except butter in saucepan; bring to boil, simmer 10 to 15 minutes, then remove from heat, stir in butter.

Banana Dessert Omelette

2 bananas,peeled, sliced
2 tablespoons apricot jam
3 tablespoons milk
1 dessertspoon sugar

3 eggs, separated
Pinch salt
3 teaspoons butter

Beat egg yolks until light & thick, add salt, stir in milk, then fold in stiffly beaten egg whites. Heat butter in large omelette pan; when sizzling pour in mixture, cook until puffy. Place banana slices on one half of omelette, spread jam over, then fold other half of omelette over; press lightly. Sprinkle with sugar, glaze under grill. Serves 2.

Banana Chocolate Popsicles

2 tablespoons orange juice
1pkt dark choc bits
1 cup finely chopped pecan nuts OR shredded coconut

3 bananas, peeled
1 tablespoon melted copha

Slice bananas in half crosswise; brush with orange juice. insert popsicle sticks in cut end of each banana half, then freeze until firm. Melt chocolate in top of double boiler, stir in copha, then cool slightly. Spoon chocolate evenly over frozen bananas, roll bananas in nuts before chocolate sets hard. Serve or wrap & keep in freezer.

Fruit Salad Pie

Pastry

2 tablespoons ground rice	1/3 cup butter
1/4 teaspoon baking powder	1 egg
1/4 cup castor sugar	1-1/2 cups flour

Cream butter & sugar, add egg, beat well. Sift flour & baking powder, then work into creamed mixture; knead until smooth, then refrigerate 30 minutes. Roll out pastry on floured surface to fit lightly greased 23cm pie plate. Trim edges, pinch to decorate.

Filling

2 bananas, peeled, sliced	1 egg
2 apples, peeled, sliced	3/4 cup sugar
2 tablespoons water	1 cup S.R. flour
1 teaspoon vanilla	3 passionfruit
1 tablespoon boiling water	Extra passionfruit
1/4 cup butter	1/4 cup milk
Pinch salt	Cream

Place apples in saucepan with 1/4 cup sugar & water; cook until just tender, then cool. Drain apples if necessary, then leave while preparing cake mixture.

Cream butter with remaining sugar & vanilla, gradually add boiling water; beat until light & fluffy; add egg, beat well. Fold in sifted flour & salt alternately with milk.

Spread apple over base of pastry in pie plate, then cover with bananas & passionfruit pulp. Sprinkle 2 tablespoons sugar over.

Spoon cake mixture over fruit, then bake in hot oven 25 to 30 minutes or until cooked. Serve with whipped cream with extra passionfruit pulp spooned over.

Banana Split

Allow for each person:

1to 2 bananas, peeled	2 scoops ice cream
Chopped mixed nuts	Whipped cream
Strawberry or chocolate topping	Glace cherries

Place banana in small dish with ice cream scoops on top. Spoon topping over ice cream, then spoon a little lightly whipped cream over this. Sprinkle nuts, garnish with cherry, serve with wafer biscuit.

Sugar Spiced Bananas

4 large bananas, peeled
Juice 1 small lemon

1/4 cup sugar
1 teaspoon cinnamon

Slice bananas lengthwise, then across. Sprinkle combined sugar & cinnamon over, then lemon juice. Serve with sweetened whipped cream or ice cream. Serves 4.

Jellied Banana Pie

3 bananas, peeled, mashed
1 pkt lemon jelly crystals
250g coconut biscuits
2 cups boiling water

Pulp 2 passionfruit
1/3 cup melted butter
Juice 1/2 lemon
Extra 1/2 banana, sliced

Stir jelly crystals in boiling water until dissolved; add lemon juice. Crush biscuits, combine crumbs with butter in bowl, then press on to base & sides of deep 23cm greased pie plate; refrigerate until firm. Add bananas & passion fruit to half jelly; refrigerate until just beginning to set, then pour into crumb crust; refrigerate until set. Arrange banana slices on top, pour over remaining jelly, then refrigerate until set. Serves 6 - 8.

Frozen Honey Cream

2 large bananas, peeled, sliced
1 dessertspoon flour
1 small orange, peeled, segmented
1/4 cup halved maraschino cherries
400g tin pineapple pieces, drained

1/2 cup honey
1 egg
1-1/4 cups cream
1 tablespoon sugar
1/3 cup lemon juice

Combine sugar, flour & honey in saucepan; bring slowly to boil. cook 1 minute, stirring. Beat egg, gradually add lemon juice, then add to honey mixture; blend well. Bring to boil, stirring, then remove from heat; cool. Add pineapple, orange, cherries & banana, then fold in whipped cream. Pour into 2 freezer trays; freeze until required. Serves 8.

Nutty Banana Ice Cream

2 ripe bananas, chopped
125g cream cheese, softened
4 tablespoons reduced cream
Little honey & chopped nuts to garnish

2 tablespoons honey
1 cup plain yoghurt
1/4 cup chopped nuts

Blend all ingredients together until smooth; place in tray, freeze until firm. Return to blender to break up ice crystals, then freeze. Serve with honey & chopped nuts.

Banana Rum Cream

3 large bananas, peeled, mashed	3/4 cup sugar
1 extra banana, peeled, sliced	2 cups cream
2 tablespoons rum	4 egg yolks
Lemon juice	1/4 cup water

Combine sugar & water in saucepan, bring to boil, cook 5 minutes then cool. Beat egg yolks in top of double saucepan; gradually stir in syrup, cooking, stirring until thick and creamy. Remove from heat, stir in mashed bananas & rum, then fold in whipped cream. Refrigerate until required; spoon into serving dishes then top with banana slices dipped in lemon juice. Serves 6.

Frozen Banana Cream

Crust

1 cup sweet biscuit crumbs	1/3 cup butter
1/4 cup ground almonds	1/4 cup castor sugar

Combine all ingredients in bowl, blending well; press onto greased base of 20cm springform pan, then refrigerate.

Banana Cream

4 eggs, separated	2 bananas
1 cup whipped cream	1/2 cup castor sugar
1 teaspoon vanilla	

Stand unpeeled bananas in bowl of iced water 1/2 hour to help maintain colour. Beat egg whites stiff, gradually add 1/2 sugar, stir in vanilla, egg yolks & peeled, mashed bananas. Whip cream with remaining sugar, then stir into mixture. Pour on prepared crumb crust, allow to freeze overnight. Serve with whipped sweetened cream, decorate with banana slices. Serves 6.

Bananas & Rum

4 firm bananas, peeled, halved crosswise	1/4 cup butter
1/4 cup packed brown sugar	Cinnamon
1/2 cup light rum	

Melt butter in frying pan over direct heat. Add bananas; sprinkle half sugar & dash cinnamon. Cook until bananas lightly browned, then turn, sprinkle sugar & cinnamon again. When soft, add rum, then set alight. Serve with pan liquid. Serves 4.

Banana Split

1 ripe banana, peeled
2 tablespoons pineapple jam
2 tablespoons chopped nuts
1 scoop each vanilla, chocolate & strawberry ice cream
1 maraschino cherry

2 tablespoons strawberry jam
2 tablespoons chocolate topping
Whipped cream

Halve banana lengthwise; put on plate cut side up. Arrange ice cream scoops in row between banana halves. Spoon strawberry jam over one scoop, pineapple over another, chocolate topping over the last. Top with cream; decorate with nuts & cherry. Makes 1 serve.

Fruity Meringue Crown

2 or 3 ripe bananas, scored, sliced diagonally
1/4 teaspoon cream of tartar
1 cup thick cream, whipped
1 to 2 cups sliced strawberries or other berries, or tinned black cherries, drained & stoned.

3/4 cup sugar
3 egg whites

Draw a 23cm circle on heavy brown paper, put on biscuit slide. Beat egg whites & cream tartar in mixer until stiff, gradually add sugar, beat until stiff & glossy. Cover circle with 12mm of mixture, then spoon remainder around edge. Bake in slow oven 1 hour. Cool; gently remove meringue from paper; put on serving plate, fill with fruit, top with whipped cream. Serves 6.

Banana & Rum Pie

6 to 8 bananas, peeled
1 tablespoon butter or margarine
1 tablespoon evaporated milk
Pastry for 23cm pie crust & top

3/4 cup sugar
1 teaspoon nutmeg
2 tablespoons light rum

Cut bananas in half then halve lengthwise. Line pan with pastry; arrange bananas over pastry. Mix sugar & nutmeg, pour over bananas. Sprinkle rum, dot with butter; top with pastry, cut few slits, then brush with evaporated milk. Bake in very hot oven 15 minutes then reduce heat, bake further 15 minutes. Serve warm or cool.

Banana Cream Layer Cake

1-1/2 cups sifted flour
Grated rind 1/2 lemon
3 ripe bananas, peeled, sliced
1 cup thick cream, whipped & sweetened
1-1/2 teaspoons double acting baking powder

1/2 teaspoon salt
3 eggs, separated
Sugar
Lemon juice & rind

Sift flour, baking powder & salt together three times. Add 3/4 cup cold water & lemon rind to egg yolks, then beat with beater or mixer until tripled in volume. Add 1 cup plus 2 tablespoons sugar a few tablespoons at a time, beating well after each addition. Add flour mixture a little at a time, beating gently & slowly with beater.

Beat egg whites until foamy, add 1-1/2 teaspoons lemon juice & 3 tablespoons sugar; continue beating until mixture peaks. Fold into flour mixture, then pour batter into 2 ungreased round 23cm layer cake pans 44mm deep. Bake in moderate oven 25 to 30 minutes. Turn upside down on cake racks then stand until cold; remove from pans. Before serving, cover with banana slices dipped in lemon juice. Top with 2nd layer; decorate with whipped cream & bananas. Or use 1 layer cut in half for smaller serve, reserving half cake for later.

Loretta's Banana Desserts

1. 3 bananas, peeled
    Juice 1/2 lemon
    1 tablespoon rum (optional)

    1 tablespoon butter
    1 tablespoon honey
    Little shredded coconut

Halve bananas lengthwise then place in greased dish. In separate pan melt butter, add lemon juice, honey & rum, then pour over bananas; top with coconut. Bake in moderate oven 20 minutes; serve hot.

2. 4 bananas, peeled
    2 eggs, beaten
    1 cup shredded coconut

    Juice 1 large lemon
    2 tablespoons sugar
    2 tablespoons apricot jam

Slice bananas diagonally, place in ovenproof dish. Sprinkle lemon juice generously. Beat together eggs & sugar until thick & creamy, then add coconut & jam; stir well. Pour over bananas, then bake uncovered in moderate oven 30 minutes or until golden brown.

Banana Meringue Pie

2 OR 3 bananas, peeled.
2-1/2 cups milk
6 tablespoons flour
3 eggs, separated
1/2 teaspoon vanilla essence
1/4 teaspoon cream of tartar

1/2 cup sugar
6 tablespoons extra sugar
1/4 teaspoon salt
1 tablespoon butter
1 baked 23cm pie shell

Mix 1/2 cup sugar, flour & salt in top of double boiler; add milk then cook, stirring, over boiling water until thickened. Cover & cook, stirring occasionally, 10 minutes. Beat egg yolks, add small amount of milk mixture slowly to yolks; return to boiler then cook, stirring 2 minutes. Remove from heat, add butter & vanilla; cool.

To prepare meringue add cream of tartar to egg whites; beat until frothy; add 6 tablespoons sugar, 1 tablespoon at a time, beating well after each. Continue beating until meringue is very stiff. Slice banana into shell then cover at once with cooled cooked mixture. Pile meringue lightly over pie, bake in hot oven 5 minutes.

Quick Banana Desserts

BANANA-NUT WHIZ : Roll banana chunks in chopped walnuts, pecans, almonds or peanuts; serve with chocolate or butterscotch topping.

BANANA & RHUBARB: Serve sliced ripe bananas with chilled stewed red rhubarb.

BANANA SUNDAE: Top a large scoop of chocolate ice cream with halved banana slices, chocolate topping & salted peanuts.

BANANAS & SOUR CREAM: Serve sliced bananas generously topped with sour cream & sprinkled with mixture of cinnamon & sugar.

BANANA TREAT: Make apricot jam sandwich with toasted slices of madiera cake. Serve with sliced banana & whipped cream topping topped with a little jam.

FRUIT BAR & BANANA PUDDING: Fill dessert bowl with crumbled spicy fruit bars & sliced bananas; top with soft whipped cream & nuts.

Banana Gingerbread Dessert

4 or 5 ripe bananas, peeled
1 pkt gingerbread mix
3 tablespoons lemon juice

1 cup sultanas
Vanilla ice cream

Sprinkle bananas with lemon juice then mash to fill 2 cups. Add to gingerbread mix; beat in mixer until well mixed, then fold in sultanas. Put in greased 6 cup ring mould; bake in moderate oven about 45 minutes. Let stand in mould 5 to 10 minutes, then unmould to serve slightly warm with ice cream filled centre. Serves 8.

Banana & Strawberry Dessert

1 pkt strawberry flavoured gelatin
1/2 cup thick cream, whipped
Additional banana slices OR fresh strawberries

Grated rind 1 lemon
4 ripe bananas, peeled, sliced

Dissolve gelatin in 1 cup boiling water, then add 1 cup cold water & lemon rind; chill until thickened but not firm, fold in cream. Make alternate layers of gelatin mixture & banana slices in parfait glasses or dessert dishes. Decorate with fruit. Serves 6.

Tropical Baked Bananas

4 slightly green-tipped bananas, peeled
1/4 cup lime juice OR lemon juice
2 tablespoons butter, melted
Dairy sour cream

1/3 cup honey
1/4 cup dry sherry
Cinnamon

Put bananas in buttered shallow baking dish, brush with lime juice. Blend honey, sherry & butter; pour over bananas. Bake in hot oven 15 to 20 minutes or until bananas are tender. Serve warm with sour cream & dusting of cinnamon. Serves 4.

Quick Banana Ice Cream

2 large, ripe bananas   2-1/2 cups vanilla ice cream, softened

Slice bananas into bowl, beat or use mixer until smooth, then beat in ice cream, one quarter at a time. Put in freezer 1 hour or until firm. If liked, 1/2 cup chopped pecans or walnuts can be folded into mixture before freezing.

Banana Milk Shake

1 ripe banana, peeled   1 cup cold milk

Slice banana into bowl, beat or use mixer until smooth, then add milk; mix well or blend. Serve at once. Makes 1 large or 2 medium serves.

Banana-Chocolate Shake: Add 1 tablespoon chocolate syrup with milk.

Banana-frosted Shake: Add small scoop vanilla ice cream before blending.

Banana Cream Pie No. 1

Pastry

2 tablespoons ground rice	1/3 cup butter
1/4 cup castor sugar	1 egg
1/4 teaspoon baking powder	1-1/2 cups flour

Cream butter & sugar, add egg, beating well. Sift flour, rice & baking powder; work into creamed mixture, kneading well until smooth. Refrigerate 30 minutes, then roll out on floured surface to fit lightly greased 23cm pie plate. Prick base & sides well with fork, use trimmings to decorate edges. Bake in hot oven 15 minutes or until lightly golden. Allow to cool.

Filling

1 tablespoon gelatine	4 bananas, sliced
2/3 cup brown sugar lightly packed	2 tablespoons butter
1/2 cup cream, lightly whipped	Lemon juice
Extra whipped cream	1 cup milk
1/2 cup water	2 eggs, separated

Combine butter, sugar & half water in saucepan, then cook & stir to dissolve sugar; cool slightly then stir in milk. Dissolve gelatine in remaining water over heat, then cool; blend into milk mixture. Add lightly beaten egg yolks, cool, when beginning to stiffen fold in cream & stiffly beaten egg whites. Dip banana slices in lemon juice, reserve some for decoration; arrange rest on base of cooked pie case. Pour cream mixture over carefully, then refrigerate until set. When ready to serve, decorate with extra whipped cream & reserved banana slices; place half glace cherry in centre. A good party dessert.

Banana Cream Pie No. 2

2 bananas, peeled, sliced
1/4 cup + 2 teaspoons cornflour
3 egg yolks, beaten
1-1/2 tablespoons butter
4 tablespoons icing sugar
1-1/2 teaspoons vanilla essence

3 cups milk
3/4 cup sugar
Pinch salt
3/4 cup thick cream
1 cooked pastry shell
(as in Banana Cream Pie 1)

Arrange banana slices in pastry shell. Put sugar in heavy pan; add cornflour & salt, mixing well. Mix egg & milk, then gradually stir into sugar mixture. Stir over heat until mixture thickens; boil 1 minute, stirring constantly. Remove from heat, then stir in butter & vanilla. Pour into pie shell over bananas, cover with waxed paper or plastic wrap. Allow to cool, then chill until firm. Whip cream until foamy, then add icing sugar, beating until it peaks. Spread over pie filling.

Banana & Rum Butterscotch Topping

1 cup lightly packed brown sugar
1/2 teaspoon nutmeg (optional)
4 slightly green tipped medium bananas

1/3 cup butter
3 tablespoons dark rum

Melt butter in pan, add sugar, nutmeg & rum; bring to boil then simmer 10 minutes. Slice bananas into mixture, stir then simmer 5 minutes or until bananas are tender. Serve warm on ice cream. Serves 6.

Banana & Cheese Pie

Pie Crust
1-2/3 cups shredded wheatmeal OR granita biscuits, crushed
1/4 cup sugar   1/4 cup plus 2 tablespoons butter, melted

Combine ingredients, mixing well; firmly press mixture evenly over bottom & sides of 23cm pie dish.

Filling
250g soft cream cheese
1 cup dairy sour cream
125g pkt vanilla instant pudding
1 cup mashed banana
1 teaspoon vanilla extract

Beat cheese until fluffy; gradually beat in sour cream, then add remaining ingredients, beat at low speed until blended. Pour into crust; chill until firm.

Baked Bananas & Honey

4 bananas, peeled
2 teaspoons melted butter
1/4 cup chopped pecan nuts

1/4 cup honey
1 tablespoon orange juice

Halve bananas crosswise, brush with butter, then place in baking dish. Add orange juice to honey, stirring well; pour over bananas. Sprinkle chopped nuts over, then bake in moderately hot oven 15 minutes. Serves 4.

Banana Pudding

6 bananas, peeled, sliced
3-1/2 tablespoons flour
2 teaspoons vanilla essence
375g pkt vanilla wafer biscuits
Extra sugar

1-1/3 cups sugar
3 eggs, separated
Pinch salt
3 cups milk

Put flour, sugar & salt in heavy pan. Beat egg yolks and mix with milk; add to pan, stirring until well mixed. Cook, stirring, on medium heat until smooth & thickened. Remove from heat, stir in 1 teaspoon vanilla essence.

In baking pan layer one third of biscuits, then cover with one third of banana slices; pour over 1/3 of custard. Repeat two more layers.

Beat egg whites until foamy; gradually add 1/3 cup extra sugar, 1 tablespoon at a time, beating until it peaks. Add rest of vanilla essence and beat until blended. Cover custard with meringue, sealing to edge of pan. Bake in moderately hot oven 10 minutes or until golden brown. Serves 8.

Flaming Bananas

4 bananas, peeled, quartered
1/4 cup packed brown sugar
1/2 teaspoon cinnamon
1 tablespoon banana OR vanilla essence

1/4 cup butter
1/4 cup white rum
Vanilla ice cream

Heat large pan to melt butter, add sugar & cinnamon, then cook over medium heat until mixture bubbles. Add bananas; heat 2 to 3 minutes, basting constantly with pan liquid; stir in banana essence. In small long handled pan warm rum, then remove from heat; light, pour over bananas, basting with syrup until flames disappear. Serve at once over ice cream.

Bananas in Almond Honey

8 bananas, peeled   100g almonds, sliced
50ml galliano liqueur   100ml honey
16 mint leaves   4 pieces alfoil

Place 2 bananas on each piece of alfoil; sprinkle with almonds. Mix honey & galliano; pour over bananas. Add mint to each, fold alfoil to secure, then cook on hotplate or barbecue about 15 minutes. Serve with ice cream.

Banana & Strawberry Crisp

3 bananas, cut in 1cm slices   1 punnet strawberries, cleaned
Deepfry batter:
    2 cups S.R. flour, sifted   1-1/2 cups water
    1/2 teaspoon bicarb
Sauce:
    100ml thick cream, whipped   500ml sour cream
    2 teaspoons icing sugar   20ml grand marnier

Combine flour, bicarb & water, mix to smooth batter. Skewer banana & strawberries, roll lightly in flour, dip in prepared batter, then deepfry. For sauce, fold sour cream into whipped cream, then sugar & grand marnier.

aby banana plants on the plantation floor

Apple & Banana Shortcake

1 egg
1 banana, sliced
1/2 cup butter
1/2 cup castor sugar
1 cup S.R. flour, sifted
Grated rind & juice 1/2 lemon

1 passionfruit
1/4 teaspoon salt
1 cup plain flour, sifted
1 tablespoon sugar
2 grated apples

Cream butter & sugar lightly; add egg, then mix in flours and salt. Divide in two, roll into rounds; place one in base of greased 20cm cake tin, then cover with apple, banana & passionfruit. Sprinkle with lemon juice & rind. Add 1 tablespoon sugar, cover with other half of dough, brush with water; sprinkle with castor sugar. Bake in moderate oven 35-40 minutes.

Crunchy Apple & Banana Pudding

3 large apples, peeled, cored, sliced
3 bananas, sliced
1 tablespoon butter
1/2 teaspoon vanilla

1/2 cup water
3 tablespoons sugar
1/2 cup sugar
1/2 cup S.R. flour

Arrange apple slices over base of pie dish, add banana slices evenly, then add water & 3 tablespoons sugar.
Mix flour, 1/2 cup sugar, vanilla & butter to resemble fine breadcrumbs; sprinkle over fruit. Bake in moderate oven 35-40 minutes or until apple is tender & top golden brown. Delicious served hot or cold with cream, ice cream or custard.

Troppo Combo Kebab

2 bananas, peeled, cut thick
2-1/2 cups fresh strawberries
100ml orange juice
200g cantaloupe, cut in chunks

1/2 pineapple, cut in chunks
100ml curacao
30g raw sugar

Using wooden skewers, make fruit kebabs, using all fruit. Mix well curacao, juice & sugar; soak kebabs in this about 4 hours, then cook on hot plate or barbecue.

Cakes

Banana Nut Bread

2 large bananas, peeled, mashed	2 eggs
1 teaspoon bicarb soda	2 cups flour
1 cup castor sugar	1/2 cup butter
1/2 cup chopped walnuts	1/3 cup milk
1 teaspoon lemon juice	1/2 teaspoon salt

Cream butter gradually adding sugar; add eggs & bananas; blend thoroughly. Sift together dry ingredients; combine milk & lemon juice; add milk mixture and dry mixture alternately, a little at a time, blending well. Stir in walnuts. Pour into 23 x 12cm greased loaf tin then bake in moderate oven 60 to 70 minutes or until cooked (test with skewer). Serve sliced with butter.

Filled & Iced Banana Cake

2 cups mashed banana	4 eggs, beaten
1 cup soft butter	3 cups sugar
3-3/4 cups plain flour	1 cup buttermilk
2 teaspoons bicarb soda	1 teaspoon vanilla essence
2 tablespoons orange juice	1 cup chopped pecans

Cream butter in mixer, adding sugar gradually; beat well then add banana, mixing until smooth, & eggs, stirring well. Mix bicarb soda into flour then add to banana mixture alternately with buttermilk, stirring well with each addition. Stir in nuts, juice & vanilla essence.

Grease & flour three 23cm round cake pans, pour batter evenly into each then bake in moderate oven 35 minutes or until inserted pick comes out clean. Cool 10 minutes in pans, then turn out onto wire racks. When quite cool spread filling between layers and over top of cake.

Banana Nut Filling

6 cups icing sugar	1/3 cup soft butter
1/2 cup mashed banana	6 cups icing sugar
2/3 cup pecans, chopped finely	4 tablespoons milk
1 cup shredded coconut, toasted	

Mix lemon juice through banana. Cream butter in mixer then add sugar & milk. Mix well then add banana mixture. Beat until fluffy then stir in nuts & coconut.

Banana Teacake

2 large ripe bananas, peeled, mashed
1 teaspoon mixed spice
2 eggs, beaten
3 tablespoons brown sugar

1/2 cup butter
1-1/2 cups S.R. flour
2 tablespoons honey

Line a greased loaf tin with baking paper. Beat butter, sugar & honey together until fluffy, then gradually beat in eggs; stir in bananas & combined spices & flour. Pour into loaf tin then bake in moderate oven 1 hour or until inserted pick comes out clean. Keeps well in airtight container.

Iced Banana Slices

1 small banana, peeled, mashed
1/4 teaspoon ground cloves
1/2 teaspoon cinnamon
1/4 cup chopped walnuts
60g butter

1 cup S.R. flour
1 egg
1/4 cup milk
1/2 cup sugar

Cream butter well; add banana, beating well 2 minutes, then add egg, beating well. Sift together flour, sugar, cloves & cinnamon; mix into banana mixture alternately with milk; stir in nuts. Place in well greased shallow baking tin; bake in moderate oven 25 minutes or until cooked. Ice while still warm. Slice and serve.

Lemon Icing

15g butter, melted
1 dessertspoon lemon juice

3/4 cup icing sugar
1 teaspoon hot water

Combine butter with lemon juice & water; blend in sifted icing sugar then mix to smooth consistency.

Banana Block Cake

1/2 cup butter
1/2 teaspoon vanilla
1/2 teaspoon bicarb soda
2 cups S.R. flour

1 cup brown sugar
2 eggs
3 bananas, peeled, mashed
1/4 cup sour milk

Cream butter & sugar; add eggs, beating well after each; add vanilla. Sift dry ingredients. Add 1/3 dry ingredients & milk to creamed mixture. Blend in 1/2 remaining dry ingredients with bananas, then add remaining dry ingredients, mixing well. Place mixture in greased swiss roll tin lined with baking paper. Bake in moderate oven 35 minutes. Allow to cool then ice top with lemon icing.

Date & Banana Slice

1-1/2 cups sliced dates
3 large bananas, peeled, sliced
1 tablespoon melted butter
1 tablespoon extra sugar
1 dessertspoon cinnamon

1/2 cup butter
1/2 cup sugar
1 cup S.R. flour
1 cup plain flour
1 egg

Cream butter & sugar together, add egg, beat until light & fluffy. Fold in sifted flours, mixing well, then press half into greased 18 X 28cm lamington tin. Cover with dates & bananas, then carefully spread remaining dough over top, pressing down lightly with floured hands. Bake in moderate oven 30 to 35 minutes or until golden brown. Brush melted butter over while hot, then sprinkle combined cinnamon & extra sugar. Good hot or cold, cut into squares. Top with whipped cream to use as dessert.

Three Layer Cake

2 cups chopped bananas
1 teaspoon baking soda
1 teaspoon cinnamon
1-1/2 teaspoons vanilla essence
Extra 1/2 cup chopped pecans
250g tin crushed pineapple

1 cup chopped pecan nuts
3 cups flour
1 teaspoon salt
3 eggs, beaten
2 cups sugar
1 cup vegetable oil

Put flour in large bowl then add soda, salt, sugar & cinnamon, mixing well. Add eggs & oil, stirring only until mixture is moistened, then stir in vanilla, pineapple (include syrup), 1 cup nuts & bananas. Pour batter into three shallow 23cm greased & floured cake tins, bake in moderate oven 25 to 30 minutes or until inserted pick comes out clean.

Allow to cool ten minutes then remove to finish cooling on wire rack.

Cream Cheese Frosting

250g cream cheese, softened
1/2 cup butter, softened

3 cups icing sugar
1 teaspoon vanilla essence

Add cream cheese to butter, beating until smooth, then add sugar & vanilla; beat until light & fluffy. Spread between layers, also on top & sides of cake, then sprinkle 1/2 cup of nuts on top. Can be refrigerated.

Iced Banana Cake

3 bananas, peeled, mashed
1 teaspoon vanilla
1 teaspoon bicarb soda
1-1/2 cups S.R. flour, sifted
Whipped cream

1 tablespoon milk
1/2 cup butter
2 eggs, beaten
1/2 cup sugar

Cream butter, sugar & vanilla; beat in eggs gradually, then add bananas. Add bicarb soda to milk, then fold into mixture alternately with flour. Bake in 2 greased & floured 18cm deep cake tins in moderate oven 25 to 30 minutes. When cold, make sandwich filled with whipped cream, top with caramel icing.

Caramel Icing

2 cups brown sugar
1/2 cup milk

1/4 cup butter

Combine ingredients in saucepan, bring to boil, stirring. Boil 5 minutes without stirring; remove from heat then beat until thick.

Banana Cream Cheese Slices

Pastry

2 tablespoons sugar
1-1/2 cups flour
1 small egg, beaten

1/3 cup butter
Pinch salt

Sift flour, sugar & salt in bowl, rub in butter, then mix to firm dough with egg. Knead on lightly floured surface, divide in 1/3 and 2/3 pieces. Reserve smaller portion, roll out larger portion to line 28 X 18cm lamington tin. Bake in moderate oven 10 minutes, then remove; allow to cool.

Filling

3 bananas, peeled, mashed
Juice & grated rind 1 lemon
1/2 cup chopped raisins
180g cream cheese, softened

1/4 cup butter
1/4 cup sugar
2 eggs, separated

Cream butter & sugar, beat in egg yolks; stir in cheese, bananas, raisins, lemon rind & juice. Beat egg whites stiff, fold into mixture, then spread over cold, partly cooked pastry. Roll out reserved pastry, cut into 25mm strips, then arrange criss cross or lattice form over filling. Glaze with little milk then bake further 20 to 25 minutes. Cool in tin, then cut in slices or squares.

Banana Loaf Cake

1/2 cup butter, softened
1 cup mashed, very ripe banana
3/4 cup loose light brown sugar
3/4 cup granulated sugar
1 teaspoon vanilla essence
1 teaspoon baking powder

1 egg
1 egg yolk
2 cups flour
3/4 cup buttermilk
1/2 teaspoon salt
1/2 teaspoon baking soda

Cream butter; gradually add sugars, beating until fluffy. Add vanilla, egg & yolk; beat well. Blend in banana then add mixed dry ingredients alternately with buttermilk, beating after each addition until smooth. Pour into well greased 23 X 12 X 8cm loaf pan; bake in slow oven 55 minutes or until done. Cool in pan on cake rack 10 minutes then turn out.

Banana & Date Loaf

4 medium bananas, peeled, mashed
2 tablespoons milk
1/2 cup dates, finely chopped
1 teaspoon bicarb soda
3/4 cup sugar

1/2 cup butter
2 eggs
2 cups S.R. flour
Pinch salt

Cream together butter & sugar until light & fluffy; add eggs, mixing well, fold in bananas. Add soda dissolved in milk, then sifted flour & salt alternately with dates. Turn into greased 23 X 12cm loaf tin; bake in moderate oven 1 hour or until cooked through. Cool on rack. Serve warm or cold, sliced, buttered.

Easy Banana Pound Cake

1 cup mashed banana
Rind 1 lemon, grated
500g madiera OR pound cake mix (omit liquid called for)

2 eggs
1/2 cup chopped nuts (optional)

Combine banana, cake mix, eggs & lemon rind in large bowl of electric mixer, blend, then beat 3 minutes medium speed; OR put in other bowl, then beat 450 strokes by hand. Fold in nuts if liked. Put in generously greased & floured 23 X 12 X 8cm loaf pan. Bake in slow oven 1-1/2 hours or until golden brown and done. Cool in pan on cake rack 30 minutes then turn out; turn right side up.

Nutty Banana Bread

1-1/2 cups mashed bananas	1-1/4 cups sugar
1/2 cup buttermilk	2 eggs
1/2 cup soft butter	2-1/2 cups S.R. flour
1 teaspoon vanilla essence	1/2 cup shredded coconut
1 cup macadamia nuts, chopped, toasted	

Preheat moderate oven; grease bottom of 23 X 12 X 8cm loaf tin. Put butter in bowl then mix in sugar, add eggs, stirring to mix thoroughly. Add buttermilk, bananas & vanilla, beating until smooth; stir in flour, then coconut & nuts. Pour into tin; bake 75 minutes or until inserted pick comes out clean. Cool 5 minutes then loosen sides to remove loaf. Slice when cold. For a variation, substitute 1/2 cup dark chocolate chips for coconut, and 1/2 cup chopped peanuts for macadamia nuts.

Banana Bread

2 medium bananas	1-1/4 cups flour
1 teaspoon baking soda	1 cup sugar
1/2 cup cooking margarine	2 eggs
1/2 teaspoon salt	

Sift dry ingredients into bowl. Whirl remaining ingredients in blender to form emulsion; add to dry ingredients, mix just until dry ingredients are moistened. Spoon into lightly buttered & floured 23cm square pan, then bake in moderate oven 35 to 40 minutes. Remove from oven, let stand in pan 5 minutes. Loosen edges with spatula, turn out on to wax paper covered rack. Cool to room temperature before cutting into squares. This is a moist, spongy bread that stays fresh several days if stored airtight.

Banana Loaf & Muffins

2 ripe bananas, peeled, mashed
1-1/4 teaspoons cream tartar
3/4 teaspoon bicarb soda
1/2 cup vegetable oil

1-3/4 cups flour
3/4 cup sugar
1 teaspoon salt
2 eggs, beaten

Put flour in large bowl, add bicarb soda, salt, sugar & cream tartar; make well in centre. Mix together eggs, oil & bananas, then add to dry mixture, stirring until moistened. Pour batter into greased 23 x 12 x 8cm loaf pan, then bake in moderate oven 45 minutes or until inserted pick comes out clean. Cool in pan 10 minutes then remove from pan; allow to cool on rack.

To make muffins, spoon batter into greased muffin pans, filling each 3/4 full. Bake in moderate oven 18 minutes or until golden brown. Remove from pans when cooked.

Scones & Biscuits

Iced Banana Biscuits

1 small banana, mashed
1/4 cup chopped almonds
1/2 cup butter
Few drops vanilla

1/2 cup icing sugar, sifted
1-1/3 cups flour, sifted
1/2 teaspoon cinnamon
Pinch salt

Cream butter, adding icing sugar; beat until light and fluffy. Blend in banana, vanilla & salt; add flour & cinnamon, mixing well, then stir in almonds; refrigerate 1 hour. Shape teaspoonsful into small balls, place on baking tray then flatten with bottom of glass (floured). Bake in moderate oven 15 to 20 minutes or until light golden brown, then cool and ice. Makes about 30.

Icing

1 teaspoon butter, melted
1 dessertspoon hot milk

1/2 cup icing sugar, sifted
Few drops vanilla

Beat all ingredients together until smooth.

Banana Crispies

1 small ripe banana, peeled, mashed	1 cup S.R. flour
1 dessertspoon powdered milk	1/3 cup castor sugar
3 tablesoons butter	1 teaspoon honey
1 dessertspoon custard powder	1/4 teaspoon salt
Pinch nutmeg	

Cream together butter & sugar until light & creamy. Add banana & honey to mixture; beat well. Fold in sifted dry ingredients then refrigerate 1 hour.

Take teaspoonfuls of mixture, roll into small balls in floured hands. Place on ungreased baking trays, press down with fork dipped in flour. Bake in moderate oven about 15 minutes or until golden brown. Makes about 24.

Banana Scones

2 cups S.R. flour	1 egg, beaten
1 cup chopped dried bananas	Pinch salt
2 teaspoons baking powder	1/3 cup milk
1 tablespoon butter	

Sift together flour, baking powder & salt; rub in butter until mixture is like fine breadcrumbs. Add dried bananas & egg, then enough milk to form soft dough. Turn out on floured board, knead lightly, then roll out 15mm thick. Cut out with floured cutter, place on greased baking tray then brush with milk. Bake in hot oven 10 to 15 minutes or until golden brown; serve hot or cold.

Banana Scrolls

1 large banana, mashed	2 cups S.R. flour
4 teaspoons soft butter	1 teaspoon cinnamon
60g cheddar cheese, grated	1 tablespoon brown sugar
3/4 cup milk	Little cinnamon sugar mixture

Rub flour into butter until like breadcrumbs; add milk, cinnamon & sugar to make soft dough. On floured surface roll out to make rectangle 35cm long, 5mm thick, then spread with banana, sprinkle cheese over. Roll up lenthwise then cut in 2.5cm slices. In buttered 23cm round cake tin, arrange scrolls in circle; brush with milk & sprinkle cinnamon sugar. Bake in preheated hot oven 35 to 40 minutes, then sprinkle icing sugar over; pull scrolls apart. Serve warm or cold with butter if liked,

PAWPAWS

Pawpaw is both a fruit and a vegetable, it can be cooked and eaten while still green. The pawpaw melon is greenish yellow to red-orange and the flesh is amber coloured when ripe. The fruit is picked during Spring and Summer, it is best when starting to turn yellow at the top, just before it is fully ripe.

It is commonly used with ice cream or cream, on its own or in fruit salads; the unripe (green) fruit can be cooked for use as a vegetable, or in pickles, chutney or jam. Pawpaw is very nutritous and is easily digested, in fact it helps the digestion of other foods it is eaten with.

Pawpaw-Banana-Nectar

1 cup mashed pawpaw	1/2 cup sugar
1 cup mashed ripe banana	2/3 cup water
1 cup canned guava juice (unsweetened)	
2 tablespoons lemon juice	

Peel ripe pawpaw and banana, cut into pieces, pass through coarse sieve. Combine all ingredients, stir to blend thoroughly, then pour over cracked ice until chilled. Makes about 4 cups.

Pawpaw Pineapple Juice

2 cups ripe pawpaw, diced	1/4 cup lemon juice
2-1/2 cups pineapple juice	1/2 cup honey

Pass pawpaw through coarse sieve, then combine with juices & honey; stir until honey dissolved. Pour over cracked ice; serve cold.

Green Pawpaw & Chicken Soup

1 medium green pawpaw	1 clove garlic, minced
1-1/2 cups chopped tomato	1 large onion, sliced
2 cups tomato juice	2 cups cooked chicken, diced
2 cups chicken stock or water	2 tablespoons cooking oil
Salt & pepper to taste	1/2 teaspoon thyme

Peel, seed, dice pawpaw. Saute onion & garlic in saucepan until golden brown, then add remaining ingredients except chicken. Cover, simmer 20 minutes or until flavours are blended; add chicken, simmer 5 minutes. Season and serve.

Green Pawpaw Soup No. 1

1 medium onion, chopped	2 tablespoons butter
1/2 teaspoon salt	1/4 teaspoon pepper
2 cups chicken stock	1 cup milk
1/4 teaspoon ground nutmeg	
1-1/2 cups pureed cooked green pawpaw	

Saute onion in butter until translucent; add salt & pepper. Remove from heat then gradually stir in stock & milk. Bring to boil, stirring constantly. Add nutmeg & pawpaw, stirring to blend in; lower heat, cook until heated through. Adjust seasonings.

VARIATION

For a thicker soup, beat 1 egg yolk with 1/4 cup milk & 1/4 cup cream; Stir some of hot soup into egg mixture then add to soup; heat but do not boil.

Cream of Pawpaw Soup

1 large green pawpaw, sliced thinly	1/2 onion, chopped
2 cups chicken stock	1/2 cup heavy cream
1/2 teaspoon dried tarragon	Salt & pepper to taste
Chopped parsley for garnish	

Cook pawpaw & onion in chicken stock until tender. Put through food mill then return to saucepan. Bring to simmer then stir in cream; season with tarragon, salt & pepper; heat through.

Serve immediately. Garnish with parsley. Can be served cold. Serves 4.

Chicken Pawpaw Soup

1 large onion, chopped	1 clove garlic, minced
2 tablespoons cooking oil	1/2 cup dried thyme
1 green pawpaw, peeled, diced	2 cups tomato juice
1-1/2 cups chopped tomatoes	2 cups diced cooked chicken
2 cups chicken stock or water	Salt & pepper to taste

Saute onion & garlic in saucepan until golden. Add remaining ingredients except chicken; simmer covered 20 minutes or until flavours blend. Add chicken then simmer 5 minutes; adjust seasonings before serving.

Green Pawpaw Soup No. 2

1 medium greeen pawpaw, peeled, cubed   1 cup chopped onion
4 cups chicken stock, heated   1 clove garlic, minced
1 cup shredded cooked chicken   2 tablespoons butter
Chopped coriander for garnish   1 tablespoon flour
1/4 teaspoon white pepper   1 teaspoon salt
Paper thin lime slices for garnish

Cook pawpaw in 2 cups boiling salted water 10 minutes or until tender. Puree in blender with cooking water then set aside.

Saute onion & garlic in butter until golden, stir in flour. When smooth add chicken stock slowly, stirring until smooth. Add puree then cook 5 minutes stirring occasionally. Add chicken, cook until heated through; add seasonings. Garnish with coriander & lime.

Green Pawpaw Dip

1 cup green pawpaw, finely grated   1 cup plain yoghurt
2 cloves garlic, minced   Salt & pepper to taste

Mix all ingredients; cover, chill. Stir before serving. Good with curry or cold meat.

Lamb Kebab with Pawpaw

500g lean lamb cut in cubes   1 cup plain yoghurt
1 garlic clove, minced   1/2 teaspoon pepper
1 teaspoon dried thyme   12 pearl onions
2 green capsicum cut in squares   Olive oil or melted butter
1 green pawpaw cut in bite size squares

Marinate meat in a mixture of yoghurt, pepper, garlic & thyme 1 hour. String lamb cubes & vegetables alternately on skewers; brush with oil or melted butter; grill, turning skewers occasionally until lamb is cooked to liking. If lamb is preferred pink, parboil vegetables 3 to 5 minutes before grilling. Serves 4.

Pawpaw Frittata

1 medium green pawpaw, grated
1 tomato, peeled, chopped
Dash of dried thyme, basil & oregano
2 tablespoons corn or peanut oil
2 tablespoons chopped fresh green chilli pepper

1 onion, chopped
1 clove garlic, minced
Salt & pepper to taste
3 eggs, beaten

Put oil in frypan then saute onion, garlic, pawpaw, tomato & seasonings until tender. Pour eggs over, stir gently; cover, cook over low heat until eggs are set. Prick puffed middle with fork. When frittata is set and browned on bottom, slide out. Invert on platter, cut in wedges to serve. Serves 6.

Olive & Tomato Pawpaw

1 large onion, sliced
3 tablespoons butter
1 teaspoon salt
1 teaspoon paprika
1 green pawpaw, quartered lengthwise, cut in 40mm lengths
1 cup pimiento stuffed green olives, sliced
2 cups tomatoes, peeled, chopped

1 clove garlic, minced
2 tablespoons flour
1/4 teaspoon pepper

Put butter in frypan then saute onion & garlic until just heated; stir in flour, seasonings & tomatoes. Cook & stir until thickened then add pawpaw; simmer covered about ten minutes. Stir in olives, heat through. Serves 6.

Avocado-Pawpaw Salad

1 ripe avocado, peeled, sliced
1 cup green pawpaw, shredded finely
12 cherry tomatoes, halved
1 head lettuce, torn in pieces
Fresh ground pepper to taste
1/4 teaspoon worcestershire

1 lemon
1/3 cup sour cream
2 teaspoons dry mustard

Squeeze lemon juice over avocado slices; chill. Mix pawpaw, tomatoes & lettuce in salad bowl. In small bowl mix sour cream, mustard, pepper & sauce; pour over salad. Place avodaco slices on top. Serves 4.

Pawpaw Cold Dish

1 teaspoon caraway seeds, crushed
1 green pawpaw, grated
1 medium cucumber, peeled, seeded, grated

1 cup plain yoghurt
1/2 teaspoon salt
1/4 teaspoon pepper

Beat yoghurt until smooth. Add remaing ingredients; mix well, then chill. Good as antipasto or served with curries.

Pawpaw Pineapple Salad

1-1/2 cups diced just green pawpaw
1 tablespoon finely chopped onion
3/4 cup mayonnaise
French dressing

1-1/2 cups diced pineapple
1 cup chopped celery
Fresh, crisp lettuce leaves

Peel pawpaw, cut in small cubes. Steam lightly about 3 minutes; drain. Marinate overnight in French dressing. Drain, combine with other ingredients; serve on lettuce leaves.

Pawpaw Banana Salad

Pawpaws (just ripe)
Juice of 1 or 2 lemons
Fresh green lettuce

Bananas (firm)
Mayonnaise

Cut bananas & pawpaws into small cubes. More or less of either can be used if preferred. Add mayonnaise & lemon juice to taste. Lay on bed of crisp green lettuce.

Italian Salad Bowl

2 cups green pawpaw sliced thinly
3 shallots, sliced
1 lettuce torn in small pieces
2 tablespoons white wine vinegar
1/2 cup crumbled blue cheese

1/2 cup sliced radishes
1 cup sliced mushrooms
1/4 cup olive oil
Salt & pepper to taste

Combine vegetables & mushrooms with salad greens in salad bowl. mix oil & vinegar; pour over salad; add seasonings then sprinkle blue cheese over top. Serves 6.

Hot Potato Pawpaw Salad

1 small pawpaw, sliced thinly	6 medium potatoes
2 tablespoons olive oil	1/4 cup chopped onion
1/4 cup chopped celery	1 garlic clove, minced
250g mortadella cut in 15mm cubes	1/4 cup water
1/2 cup red wine vinegar	1/2 teaspoon sugar
1 teaspoon salt	1/8 teaspoon paprika
1/4 teaspoon dry mustard	

Cook potatoes in jackets in covered pan until tender; peel & slice while hot, then keep warm. Steam pawpaw ten minutes, drain, keep warm. Heat oil in skillet then saute onion, celery, garlic & mortadella, stirring frequently until onion is golden. Stirring, combine remaining ingredients in saucepan; bring to boil then pour into skillet. Combine hot dressing with potatoes and squash, mixing gently. Serves 4 to 6.

Tuna & Pawpaw Salad

1 medium green pawpaw, shredded	1 250g tin tuna
2 small carrots, shredded	1/3 cup mayonnaise
1 teaspoon dijon style mustard	1/4 teaspoon celery salt
Freshly ground pepper	Lettuce leaves
Thinly sliced salad onion	Tomato slices (optional)

Drain tuna, then flake, place in bowl with pawpaw & carrots. In 2nd bowl combine mayonnaise, mustard & celery salt; add dressing to tuna mixture; mix lightly.

Serve on individual salad plates with lettuce leaves; sprinkle pepper over. Surround with tomato & onion slices.

Scallops with Pawpaw

3/4 cup fine fresh bread crumbs	1 teaspoon salt
1 tablespoon fresh lemon juice	1 egg
500g scallops	1 teaspoon water
Hot buttered toast	75g butter
1/4 cup chopped parsley	Lemon wedges
1 medium pawpaw, peeled, seeded, cut in 5mm slices	

Mix salt into bread crumbs. Beat egg with water & lemon juice. Roll scallops & pawpaw in crumbs, dip in egg mixture, then dip again in crumbs. Heat butter in skillet, then cook scallops & pawpaw 5 minutes or until browned & tender; sprinkle parsley, garnish with lemon. Serves 4.

Pawpaw Boats & Lamb Stuffing

2 medium firm pawpaw
750g ground lamb
2 tablespoons chopped parsley
1/2 teaspoon minced garlic
1/4 teaspoon dried rosemary
1/4 cup grated swiss cheese

1/4 cup ground almonds
1 tablespoon tomato paste
1/2 teaspoon salt
1/4 teaspoon pepper
1 egg, beaten

Saute ground lamb to taste. Seed & halve pawpaws, drop into boiling water then cook 8 to 10 minutes or until almost tender. Cool, scoop out pulp leaving 10mm thick shell, mash pulp then combine with lamb and remaining ingredients except cheese. Adjust seasoning. Divide evenly then place mixture evenly in shells. Place in shallow buttered baking dish, sprinkle cheese over top then bake uncovered in moderate oven 30 minutes. Serves 4.

Green Pawpaw Italiano

2 kg green pawpaw, seeded, peeled & coarsely grated

MEAT SAUCE

1 clove garlic, minced
1/2 cup olive oil
1/2 cup tomato paste
1-1/2 teaspoons salt
1/4 teaspoon dried basil
5 large mushrooms, slivered
2 cups Roma tomatoes, peeled, chopped

1/2 cup chopped onion
500g ground beef
1/2 cup beef stock
1/4 teaspoon pepper
1 bay leaf

Steam grated pawpaw 5 to 10 minutes while making sauce.

Saute garlic & onion in olive oil in large skillet until onion is translucent; add meat then brown lightly. Drain fat, add remaining ingredients then simmer uncovered 1 hour. Pour half sauce over pawpaw; serve remainder on side. Serves 6 to 8.

Peppy

Seasoning made from pawpaw seeds.
Makes about 1/4 cup

Save seeds from pawpaw, wash clean under running water, holding seeds in sieve. When dry, spread seeds in single layer on biscuit slide; bake in moderate oven 1-1/2 hours or until seeds resemble pepper corns. Use in pepper mill.

Lamb Chops in Foil

8 lamb loin chops
1 small green pawpaw
75g fetta or swiss cheese, sliced
3 tablespoons fresh lemon juice

Salt & pepper
3 shallots, chopped
2 cloves garlic, minced
75g butter

Season lamb chops well both sides, then put on large square of heavy foil. Peel, seed pawpaw, cut in 8 pieces. Place one piece on each chop; add slice of cheese, sprinkle onions, garlic, lemon juice, then dot with butter. Fold foil tightly at tops & sides; bake in moderate oven 1 hour or grill over charcoal, turning once. Serves 4.

Pawpaw with Meatballs

1/2 cup day old bread crumbs
1 large onion, chopped
1 garlic clove, minced
Salt & pepper to taste
2 tomatoes, peeled, chopped
1/4 cup grated parmesan cheese
2 cups freshly grated corn kernels

1/2 cup milk
250g ground pork
250g ground veal
1/2 teaspoon salt
1kg pawpaw, cubed
2 tablespoons butter

Soak bread crumbs in milk; add meats & 1/2 teaspoon salt then form meatballs the size of a marble. Brown meatballs in skillet, remove, set aside. In same pan saute pawpaw, onion & garlic in butter until onion is translucent. Add tomatoes, corn & seasoning, then add meatballs. Put in buttered casserole; bake 20 minutes in moderate oven. Sprinkle cheese on top then bake until cheese is melted. Serves 6.

Greek style Chicken & Pawpaw

1.5 kg chicken, cut in pieces
2 tomatoes, peeled, chopped
1 pawpaw, peeled, seeded, cubed
500g mushrooms, quartered

Salt & pepper
1 small eggplant, cubed
2 garlic cloves, minced
1 teaspoon dried oregano

Sprinkle chicken pieces with salt & pepper then place in shallow buttered baking dish. Bake in hot oven 15 minutes or until browned; pour off any fat. Combine all other ingredients and spoon over chicken. Bake, covered, in moderate oven 45 minutes or until tender.

Paw Paw plantations in tropical Queensland

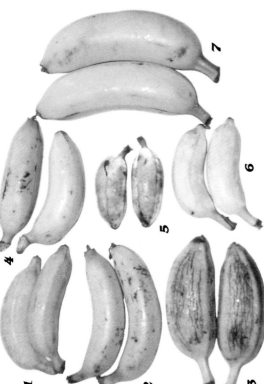

Banana Varieties

1. **Green & Red Dacca.** Excellent eating banana from P.N.G. & West Irian.
2. **Cavendish.** The common Australian banana.
3. **Ash Plantain.** Has to be eaten on the day it is ripe. Excellent as a baked vegetable with curry. Well known in the Philippines.
4. **Pisang Rajah.** Pinky tinted flesh. Eating banana well known in India, Pakistan & Malaysia.
5. **Blue Java.** Indonesia. Rather bland, eaten cooked.
6. **Ducasse or Sugar.** Sweet eating, excellent drying, good in fruit salad.
7. **Pacific Plantain.** Fiji. All purpose banana; does not oxidise or lose colour, keeps refrigerated up to two weeks. Can be used fresh, in salads, grilled, BBQ'd, dried, and in jam.
8. Ron Berry shows tropical fruits to tourists at High Falls Farm.

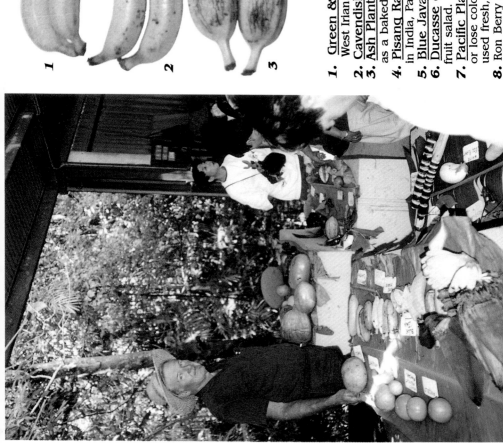

Chicken with Green Pawpaw

1.5 kg chicken pieces	4 tablespoons butter
1 clove garlic, minced	Salt & pepper to taste
1 cup chicken stock	1 egg, beaten
500g pawpaw, thinly sliced	Juice 1/4 fresh lemon

Brown chicken pieces in garlic butter; add salt, pepper & stock; simmer 20 minutes. Add pawpaw, continue cooking 10 minutes or until tender. Remove chicken & pawpaw to warm platter. Beat together lemon juice & egg; add some of pan juices while slowly beating. Return mixture to pan; heat until sauce thickened, then pour over chicken & pawpaw. Serves 6.

Ham & Pawpaw Casserole

1 small pawpaw, diced	1/2 cup cooked rice
1 leek with some green tops	2 eggs, beaten
1 cup chopped cooked ham	1/2 teaspoon salt
3/4 cup grated swiss cheese	1/4 teaspoon pepper
1/4 cup soft w/grain bread crumbs	2 tablespoons butter, melted

Combine rice, pawpaw, leek, ham, eggs, seasoning & 1/2 cup cheese. Put in buttered casserole then sprinkle remaining cheese, butter & bread crumbs; bake in moderate oven 40 minutes.

Mushrooms, Ham & Pawpaw

2 small green pawpaw	1 onion, chopped
250g mushrooms, chopped	3 tablespoons butter
1 cup diced cooked ham	1/2 teaspoon salt
1 teaspoon fresh lemon juice	1/4 teaspoon pepper
2 tablespoons chopped parsley	Dash cayenne pepper

Seed & cut pawpaw in half; drop in boiling water, cook until almost tender. Cool, scoop out pulp leaving 10mm thick shell. Saute onion & mushrooms in butter; add ham, seasoning & pulp; mix well. Place mixture in shells in shallow buttered baking dish. Bake in moderate oven 25 minutes. Serves 4.

Baked Ratatouille

A French vegetable stew

2 large cloves garlic, minced or mashed
1 medium eggplant, cut in 10mm cubes
2 red capsicum, cut in chunks
4 large tomatoes, cut in chunks
Optional: sliced tomato, parsley sprigs
2 medium pawpaw, peeled, seeded, thickly sliced

2 large onions, sliced
1 teaspoon basil
1/2 cup minced parsley
4 tablespoons olive oil
Salt to taste

Layer onions, garlic, eggplant, pawpaw, capsicum & tomatoes in a casserole; sprinkle salt, basil & parsley between layers. Press down to fit casserole if necessary; drizzle top with olive oil. Cover then bake in moderate oven 3 hours. Baste top occasionally with some of liquid; uncover during last hour of cooking if ratatouille is quite soupy (if preferred, cover can be left off to let juices cook down). Remove from oven then mix gently; add salt to taste. Serve hot, cold or reheated with parsley sprigs & tomato slices. Flavour best after standing awhile. A great salad. Serves 8 – 10.

Kidney-Pawpaw Casserole

3 veal kidneys OR 6 lamb kidneys
1 cup hot chicken or veg stock
250g mushrooms, sliced
1 tablespoon minced parsley
1/4 cup dry sherry or white wine
1/4 teaspoon freshly ground pepper

1/2 teaspoon paprika
2 tablespoons butter
1 tablespoon minced onion
1-1/2 cups diced pawpaw
1/2 teaspoon salt
Hot toast

Trim fat & white tissue from kidneys; cut into dice then drop in boiling stock; simmer 3 minutes. Remove, drain, place in heated casserole, dust with paprika. Reserve stock; keep hot. Melt butter in skillet, then saute pawpaw, mushrooms, onion & parsley, stirring, about 2 minutes; stir in flour then add hot stock. Bring to boil; cook & stir 2 minutes or until thickened. Add sherry & seasonings.

Pour over kidneys, cover casserole then bake 20 minutes in moderate oven. Serve on hot toast. Serves 4.

Tender Meat Marinade

Because papain works on exposed surfaces of meat, it will make small pieces more tender than whole roasts. This basic recipe is suitable for stewing meat.

1 ripe pawpaw, seeded, mashed	Peppy to taste
1/2 teaspoon ascorbic acid	1-1/2 cups water
1/2 teaspoon crushed dried rosemary	1-2 teaspoons cooking oil

Put oil, acid, rosemary & generous amount of peppy in water, mix well. To use, place cubed meat in shallow dish then cover with marinade, stirring well to cover all surfaces. Stand 1 hour before cooking. Drain marinade to use as base for stew gravy. Tenderising action will cause meat to cook faster.

Variation

Replace rosemary with any other dried herb.

For roasts or poultry, reduce water to 1/2 cup to make marinade consistency of jam; spread it on roasts, whole poultry or poultry pieces. It also can be injected into meat. Marinate 1.5 kg roast 2 hours; cook with liquid in dish.

Tenderising Squid & Octopus

Prepare as desired then cross hatch fillets in both directions by cutting half way into surface with sharp knife about every 10mm. Marinate overnight.

Glazed Pawpaw Slices

Ripe pawpaw	Honey
Brown sugar	Butter

Peel, seed, cut pawpaw in wide slices. Lay evenly in flat baking dish; baste with honey & butter warmed together. Sprinkle brown sugar very lightly. Cook in medium to hot oven until thoroughly cooked & nicely browned; serve from baking dish.

Brown sugar, butter & water are used for glazing sliced pawpaw, carrots & sweet potatoes, and can be used instead of honey mixture.

For a supreme flavour 1/2 cup of guava, kumquat or strawberry jam, 4 tablespoons butter & 3 tablespoons lime can be blended together then used for basting pawpaw slices until soft and glazed.

Veal'n Green Pawpaw

150g green pawpaw, diced   500g veal rump, diced
Fresh tomato sauce

Marinade - Mix together:
200ml pineapple juice, reduced to 100ml   25ml white vinegar
1 teaspoon chopped fresh mint   3 teaspoons honey
Salt & cracked black pepper to taste

Batter:
100g plain flour   150ml water
1 teaspoon baking powder   1 egg
Ground ginger   Salt

Place meat & fruit on skewers, then marinate 12 hours.
Meanwhile, whisk together batter ingredients; let stand.
Heat fat in deep fryer, remove kebabs from marinade,
shaking off excess. Dust with flour, then coat with batter
and deepfry. Serve with fresh tomato juice.

Pawpaw Boats with Coconut

3 small pawpaw   100g grated coconut
100g unsalted cashew nuts   30ml dark rum
50ml coconut milk   4 teaspoons brown sugar

Cut 2 pawpaw in half, remove seeds. Peel 3rd pawpaw,
cut in bite size pieces, then mix with other ingredients.
Fill pawpaw halves with mixture. Bake in moderate oven
or barbecue with lid over 10-15 minutes, then serve.

Pawpaw & Melon Jam

1kg pawpaw, peeled, diced
1kg Rock or Honeydew melon, peeled, diced
2kg sugar   25g chopped ginger

Place all ingredients in large pan with a little water to
keep fruit from sticking to pan when cooking begins.
Boil, stirring, until the jam is set (test by putting a dollop
onto a very cold plate; when jam is cold push with finger
- if it crinkles, it's jelled). Bottle and store in freezer or in
cool, dry cupboard.

Pawpaw with Pears

2 fresh pears, peeled, cored, chopped   2 tablespoons butter
1/2 teaspoon ground cinnamon   1/4 teaspoon salt
1 tablespoon honey   1 tablespoon sherry
2 medium pawpaws, halved lengthwise, seeded

Put pawpaw, cut side down, in shallow baking dish with hot water to 25mm. Bake in moderate hot oven 20 minutes. Saute pear, add salt, cinnamon, honey & sherry. After initial baking turn over pawpaw halves; mound pear mixture in centres, then bake in moderate oven 20 to 30 minutes longer. Serves 4.

Pawpaw Mango Mousse

1 cup ripe pawpaw pulp   1 cup ripe mango pulp
2 tablespoons lemon juice   6 tablespoons sugar
1/2 cup evaporated milk

Peel pawpaw & mangoes; press through sieve. Add sugar & lemon juice; put aside until sugar is dissolved. Use refrigerator freezer to chill evaporated milk until small crystals appear around sides of cup; pour into chilled bowl then whip until stiff. Fold in the mango-pawpaw mixture. Pour into freezer trays; freeze 4 to 6 hours.

Orange Pawpaw

3 tablespoons butter, softened   Salt to taste
3 small nearly ripe pawpaws   2 tablespoons brown sugar
2 oranges, peeled, sectioned   2 tablespoons butter
1/4 cup slivered toasted almonds

Halve pawpaws lengthwise, remove seeds & fibres, butter inside surfaces then sprinkle salt lightly. Place orange sections in each half; sprinkle brown sugar, almonds & soft butter. Put in shallow baking dish with hot water to 25mm, then bake in moderate oven 1 hour. Add water if needed while cooking. Serves 6.

Guide to Tropical Fruit

Giving the common name, origin, and interesting features.

Supplied by High Falls Farm Display Orchard, Miallo, FNQ.

Jakfruit (India) Mainly used as vegetable, fried, roasted or boiled. Ripe fruit eaten as dessert. Has strong flavour.

Miraclefruit (West Africa) Works on sour receptors of taste buds. Turns all sour tasting foods sweet. Effect lasts about 30 minutes.

Cedar Bay Cherry (North QLD) Red-brown Cherry size, pleasant flavour.

Peach Palm (Amazon, South America) Fruits have orange, starchy flesh. Eaten after prolonged boiling. The heart of palm is also edible.

Salak Palm (Asiatic Tropics) Fruit eaten fresh. Creamy yellow white colour, inside brown scaly skin; sweet acid flavour suggestive of pineapples.

Araca (South America) Very sour fruit; makes a superbly refreshing drink.

Grumichana (Brazil) Eaten fresh & used to make cakes, jellies, jams, pies.

Brazil Cherry (Brazil) Eaten fresh. Juicy & aromatic flesh.

Malay Apple (Malaysia) Pear shaped fruit, aromatic scent & pleasant taste.

Sapodilla (Central America) Grown in most equatorial areas. Has soft white flesh with slight caramel taste.

Star Apple (West Indies, Central America) Sweet white, semi translucent flesh. Eaten fresh or made into drinks, sorbets & jams.

White Sapote (Central America) Used to dilate blood vessels, reduce blood pressure & induce sleep. Used in milkshakes, ices, sorbets, fruit salad.

Santol (Malaysia, Indonesia, Philippines, South China) Juicy, thirst quenching. Flesh clings to seeds. Also used in preserves & jams.

Kwalmuk (South China) Orange fruit with uses similar to Jakfruit.

Akee (West Africa) Creamy white flesh that surrounds seeds is eaten. Resembles scrambled eggs when cooked & served on toast. Immature & overripe fruit is poisonous.

Inga (Central & South America) Sweet juicy pulp resembles ice-cream.

Durian (Malaysia, Indonesia) Has a rather strong odour. Usually eaten fresh or made into drinks.

Camu Camu (Amazon Basin) High in vitamin C. Used in drinks & organic vitamin C tablets. Has acid flesh similar to Limes.

Psidium (Central America) Type of Guava with similar eating qualities.

Rollinia (South America) 'Custard Apple' Sweet, juicy, creamy white flesh.

Ablu (South America) Very sweet, juicy, creamy white flesh. Eaten fresh.

Black Sapote (Mexico) 'Chocolate Pudding Fruit' Dark chocolate brown flesh. Has rich, sweet flavour. Good in mousses & ice-cream. High in vitamin C, calcium & phosphorous.

Marang (Borneo) Close relative of Breadfruit. Has edible pulp, sweet, juicy, fibreless & melting in texture.

Langsat (SE Asia) Refreshing, aromatic, white translucent flesh. Grows in bunches of 15-25. Eaten fresh or in salads.

Lychee (China) Early maturing, excellent eating.

Acerola (West Indies, Central America) Exceptionally rich source of vitamin C, 20-50 times that of an orange. Eaten raw or used in drinks, jellies, jams.

Bread Nut (SE Asia) Fruit used for cooking. Larger tree than Breadfruit.

Canistel (Central America) Eaten fresh with dash of lime or lemon juice. Can have consistency of hard boiled egg.

Mamey Apple (Central-South America) Oval shape with reddish orange to pink flesh. Aromatic, fibre free; good in ice cream, milkshakes & sorbets.

Dawa (South Pacific) Edible flesh similar to a Longan.

Yellow Mangosteen (SE Asia) Very acidic, opposite to purple mangosteen. Ideal for drinks

Avocado-Sharwill (Central & South America) Popular fruit discovered by the Spanish Conquistadors growing extensively throughout Central & S America.

Ambarella (Polynesia) Ripe fruit eaten fresh or made into drinks & jams. Unripe fruit is used in pickles, relishes & salads.

Custard Apple (Central & S America) Possibly cultivated since Pre-historic Peru, this very sweet fruit is best eaten fresh with a spoon.

Carambola (Malaysia & Indonesia) Eaten fresh it is crisp & refreshing, or it is used in juices. Very ripe fruit has a slightly perfumed smell.

Jaboticaba (Southern Brazil) Very sweet & slightly aromatic. Makes excellent wine and jams.

Soursop (Central American Tropics) Slightly acidic taste. Makes wonderful ice creams, sorbets & custards.

Breadfruit (SE Asia) An important basic food of SE Asia. More usually eaten as a vegetable, baked in ground ovens or over hot coals. Can be cooked in same way as potatoes. Makes excellent chips.

Rambutan (Malaysia and Sumatra) Named after malay word *Rambut*, meaning hair of head. Flavour is similar to that of Lychee.

Macadamia (Queensland) A hard nut to crack but once inside the reward is a delicious creamy kernel.

Wax Jambu (West Malaysia) Has edible flesh that is crisp, succulent, and slightly aromatic though rather tasteless.

Rollinia (Amazon River Regions) Unique yellow & black fruit. Eaten fresh with spoon. It has a very sweet, creamy white flesh.

Longan (China to India) Known as the little brother of the Lychee, they have a slightly musky, spicier flavour.

Clove (Malaysia) The flowers are dried and used as a spice.

Mango-Bowen and Mango-Peach (SE Asia) Known to have been cultivated in India for over 4000 years. There are more than 500 known varieties. The Bowen variety is stringless.

Banana (Dwarf) (Asia) One of the oldest known fruits with a high food value.

Uvilla (Western Amazon) Has large bunches of purple/black grape-like fruits.

Purple Mangosteen (SE Asia) The queen of tropical fruits has an exquisite flavour. Eaten fresh or can be made into sorbets.

Mamey Sapote (Central America) Pink sweet flesh used mainly in drinks.

South American Sapote (S America) Same family as Durian, but has sweet orange-yellow pulp with a flavour similar to rock melon.

West Indian Lime (West Indies) Makes excellent refreshing drinks.

Coffee (Ethiopia) Produces red berries which take 7 to 9 months to mature, when they are processed and ground.

Bush Lemon (Obscure) Throwback from pure strains.

Tamarind (Savannah areas of Africa) Introduced into Australia 100 years ago. Used in curries & chutneys as it has a sweet/acid pulp.

Lemon Guava (Central American Tropics) A sweet fruit usually eaten fresh but is also made into jellies and jams. Spanish and Portuguese explorers spread this fruit world wide.

Strawberry Guava (Central America) A red variety of Guava.

Passionfruit (yellow) (Brazil) The yellow variety is not as acidic as the more common purple.

Paw Paw (Papaya) (Central America) The juice and leaves are used as a meat tenderiser. Can be cooked when green but is more commonly used as dessert fruit.

Cassava or Sago Tree (Pacific Islands) A basic food in Pacific and other tropical areas. Has a high starch content.

<u>Wild Ginger</u> (Australia) Fruit can be eaten.
<u>Taro-Dryland</u> (Tropical America) A root vegetable with high starch content.
Grows in dry conditions. <u>Taro-Wetland</u> likes swampy areas.
<u>Rosellas</u> (Pacific Islands) Acid flavour. Main uses as jam, cordial and sauces.
<u>Cacao</u> (Tropical America) The Chocolate Tree. Produces beans which are
ground to produce cocoa.
<u>Lemon Grass</u> When cut and infused in boiling water it makes a very
refreshing tea.
<u>Pineapple</u> (S America) Grown from tops, slips, and lately, tissue culture.
<u>Okra</u> (Asia, Africa) Used for cooking and as a salad vegetable.
<u>Aloe Vera</u> (Central America) Wonder plant with healing capacities.
<u>Ginger</u> (S Asia) Numerous uses. Mostly used ground to powder.
<u>Granadilla</u> Giant Passionfruit.
<u>Dwarf Coconut</u> (Pacific Islands) First fruit set 1 metre above ground level.

Two Chutneys

1 Banana Chutney:

8 bananas, peeled, chopped	1-1/2 cups dates, pitted
3 small brown onions, chopped	1 tablespoon raisins
3 tablespoons dessicated coconut	1 cup coconut milk
2 teaspoons chopped mint	1/4 teaspoon cayenne
1/2 teaspoon mustard powder	1/2 teaspoon paprika
1/2 teaspoon cinnamon	1/2 cup lemon juice

Put dates & raisins in pan with lemon juice. Bring just
to boil, then reduce heat; simmer covered until absorbed
juice swells the fruit, then allow to cool. Place bananas
in blender with dates, raisins, remaining juice & all other
ingredients, then blend until well mixed. Refrigerate
overnight then bottle.

2. Pawpaw & Plum Chutney

1kg ripe pawpaw, peeled, seeded, cubed	1-3/4 cups sugar
1kg plums, pitted, cut in large chunks	1-1/2 teaspoons salt
2 tablespoons crystallised ginger, chopped	5cm cinnamon stick
1-1/4 cups cider vinegar	1/2 cup sultanas
1/8 teaspoon cayenne pepper	

Mix thoroughly in large pan all ingredients except
pawpaw & plums; Bring to boil then reduce heat;
simmer, stirring frequently until thickened. Add pawpaw
& plums; simmer, stirring, 30 minutes. Take out
cinnamon, cool, then bottle.

Some Quick Cup Measures

1 cup of:

flour	150g	fresh breadcrumbs	60g
white sugar	210g	dry breadcrumbs	125g
icing sugar	150g	biscuit crumbs	105g
brown sugar	150g	rice, raw	180g
butter	210g	mixed fruit	185g
honey	360g	nuts, chopped	125g
coconut, dried	90g	cheddar cheese, grated	150g

Measures

LIQUID		SOLID	
Imperial	Metric	Ounces	Grams
1 teaspoon	5ml	1oz	30g
1 tablespoon	20ml	4oz (1/4lb)	125g
2 fluid oz (1/4 cup)	62.5ml	8oz (1/2lb)	250g
4 fluid oz (1/2 cup)	125ml	12oz (3/4lb)	375g
8 fluid oz (1 cup)	250ml	16oz (1lb)	500g
1 pint (20 fluid oz/2½ cups)	625ml	24oz (1½lb)	750g
1 pint (US & Canada) (16 fluid oz)	500ml	32oz (2lb)	1kg

Cake Tins

6 inch - 15 cm
7 inch - 18 cm
9 inch - 23 cm

Loaf Tin: 9" x 5" - 23 x 12 cm
Bar Tin: 10" x 3" - 25 x 8 cm
Lamington: 11" x 7" - 28 x 18 cm

Oven Temperature Guide

	Electric		Gas		
	°C	°F	°C	°F	Mark
Cool	110	225	100	200	1/4
Very Slow	120	250	120	250	1/2
Slow	150	300	150	300	1 - 2
Moderately Slow	170	340	160	325	3
Moderate	200	400	180	350	4
Moderately Hot	220	425	190	375	5 - 6
Hot	230	450	200	400	6 - 7
Very Hot	250	475	230	450	8 - 9

CUP AND SPOON EQUIVALENTS IN OUNCES & GRAMS

INGREDIENT	1/2oz 15g	1oz 30g	2oz 60g	3oz 90g	4oz 125g	5oz 150g	6oz 180g	7oz 210g	8oz 250g
Almonds:									
ground	2T	1/4C	1/2C	3/4C	1-1/4C	1-1/3C	1-2/3C	2C	2-1/4
Apples, dried	3T	1/2C	1C	1-1/3C	2C	2-1/3C	2-3/4C	3-1/3C	3-3/4
Apricots:									
chopped	2T	1/4C	1/2C	3/4C	1C	1-1/4C	1-1/2C	1-3/4C	2C
whole	2T	3T	1/2C	2/3C	1C	1-1/4C	1-1/3C	1-1/2C	1-3/4
Arrowroot	1T	2T	1/3C	1/2C	2/3C	3/4C	1C	1-1/4C	1-1/3
Baking Pdr	1T	2T	1/3C	1/2C	2/3C	3/4C	1C	1C	1-1/4
Barley	1T	2T	1/4C	1/2C	2/3C	3/4C	1C	1C	1-1/4
Bicarb. Soda	1T	2T	1/3C	1/2C	2/3C	3/4C	1C	1C	1-1/4
Breadcrumbs:									
dry	2T	1/4C	1/2C	3/4C	1C	1-1/4C	1-1/2C	1-3/4C	2C
soft	1/4C	1/2C	1C	1-1/2C	2C	2-1/2C	3C	3-2/3C	4-1/4
Biscuit Crumbs	2T	1/4C	1/2C	3/4C	1-1/4C	1-1/3C	1-2/3C	2C	2-1/4
Butter	3t	6t	1/4C	1/3C	1/2C	2/3C	3/4C	1C	1C
Cheese grated:									
nat. cheddar	6t	1/4C	1/2C	3/4C	1C	1-1/4C	1-1/2C	1-3/4C	2C
proc. cheddar	5t	2T	1/3C	2/3C	3/4C	1C	1-1/4C	1-1/2C	1-2/3
Parmesan and									
Romano	6t	1/4C	1/2C	3/4C	1C	1-1/3C	1-2/3C	2C	2-1/4
Cherries glace									
chopped	1T	2T	1/3C	1/2C	3/4C	1C	1C	1-1/3C	1-1/2
whole	1T	2T	1/3C	1/2C	2/3C	3/4C	1C	1-1/4C	1-3/4
Cocoa	2T	1/4C	1/2C	3/4C	1-1/4C	1-1/3C	1-2/3C	2C	2-1/4
Coconut, dried	2T	1/3C	2/3C	1C	1-1/3C	1-2/3C	2C	2-1/3C	2-2/3
shredded	1/3C	2/3C	1-1/4C	1-3/4C	2-1/2C	3C	3-2/3C	4-1/3C	5C
Cornflour	6t	3T	1/2C	2/3C	1C	1-1/4C	1-1/2C	1-2/3C	2C
Coffee: ground	2T	1/3C	2/3C	1C	1-1/3C	1-2/3C	2C	2-1/3C	2-2/3
instant	3T	1/2C	1C	1-1/3C	1-3/4C	2-1/4C	2-2/3C	3C	3-1/2
Cornflakes	1/2C	1C	2C	3C	4-1/4C	5-1/4C	6-1/4C	7-1/3C	8-1/3
Cream of Tartar	1T	2T	1/3C	1/2C	2/3C	3/4C	1C	1C	1-1/4
Currants	1T	2T	1/3C	2/3C	3/4C	1C	1-1/4C	1-1/2C	1-2/3
Custard Powdr.	6t	3T	1/2C	2/3C	1C	1-1/4C	1-1/2C	1-2/3C	2C
Dates, choppd	1T	2T	1/3C	2/3C	3/4C	1C	1-1/4C	1-1/2C	1-2/3
whole, pitted	1T	2T	1/3C	1/2C	3/4C	1C	1-1/4C	1-1/3C	1-1/2
Figs, chopped	1T	2T	1/3C	1/2C	3/4C	1C	1C	1-1/3C	1-1/2
Flour, SR, plain	6t	1/4C	1/2C	3/4C	1C	1-1/4C	1-1/2C	1-3/4C	2C
wholemeal	6t	3T	1/2C	2/3C	1C	1-1/4C	1-1/3C	1-2/3C	1-3/4
Fruit, mixed	1T	2T	1/3C	1/2C	3/4C	1C	1-1/2C	1-1/3C	1-1/2
Gelatine	5t	2T	1/3C	1/2C	3/4C	1C	1C	1-1/4C	1-1/2
Ginger:									
crystalised	1T	2T	1/3C	1/2C	3/4C	1C	1-1/4C	1-1/3C	1-1/2
ground	6t	1/3C	1/2C	3/4C	1-1/4C	1-1/2C	1-3/4C	2C	2-1/4
in syrup	1T	2T	1/3C	1/2C	2/3C	3/4C	1C	1C	1-1/4
Glucose, liquid	2t	1T	2T	1/4C	1/3C	1/2C	1/2C	2/3C	2/3
Golden Syrup	2t	1T	2T	1/4C	1/3C	1/2C	1/2C	2/3C	2/3
Haricot Beans	1T	2T	1/3C	1/2C	2/3C	3/4C	1C	1C	1-1/4

t = teaspoonful   T = tablespoonful   C = cupful

CUP AND SPOON EQUIVALENTS IN OUNCES & GRAMS

INGREDIENT	1/2oz 15g	1oz 30g	2oz 60g	3oz 90g	4oz 125g	5oz 150g	6oz 180g	7oz 210g	8oz 250g
Honey	2t	1T	2T	1/4C	1/3C	1/2C	1/2C	2/3C	2/3C
Jam	2t	1T	2T	1/4C	1/3C	1/2C	1/2C	2/3C	3/4C
Lentils	1T	2T	1/3C	1/2C	2/3C	3/4C	1C	1C	1-1/4C
Macaroni	1T	2T	1/3C	2/3C	3/4C	1C	1-1/4C	1-1/2C	1-2/3C
Milk Powder:									
full cream	2T	1/4C	1/2C	3/4C	1-1/4C	1-1/3C	1-2/3C	2C	2-1/4
non fat	2T	1/3C	3/4C	1-1/4C	1-1/2C	2C	2-1/3C	2-3/4C	3-1/4C
Nutmeg	6t	3T	1/2C	2/3C	3/4C	1C	1-1/4C	1-1/2C	1-2/3C
Nuts, chop'd	6t	1/4C	1/2C	3/4C	1C	1-1/4C	1-1/2C	1-3/4C	2C
Oatmeal	1T	2T	1/2C	2/3C	3/4C	1C	1-1/4C	1-1/2C	1-2/3C
Olives whole	1T	2T	1/3C	2/3C	3/4C	1C	1-1/4C	1-1/2C	1-2/3C
sliced	1T	2T	1/3C	2/3C	3/4C	1C	1-1/4C	1-1/2C	1-2/3C
Pasta, short	1T	2T	1/3C	2/3C	3/4C	1C	1-1/4C	1-1/2C	1-2/3C
Peaches:									
dried whole	1T	2T	1/3C	2/3C	3/4C	1C	1-1/4C	1-1/2C	1-2/3C
chopped	6t	1/4C	1/2C	3/4C	1C	1-1/4C	1-1/2C	1-3/4C	2C
Peanuts:									
shelled raw	1T	2T	1/3C	1/2C	3/4C	1C	1-1/4C	1-1/3C	1-1/2C
roasted	1T	2T	1/3C	2/3C	3/4C	1C	1-1/4C	1-1/2C	1-2/3C
Peanut Butter	3t	6t	3T	1/3C	1/2C	1/2C	2/3C	3/4C	1C
Peas, split	1T	2T	1/3C	1/2C	2/3C	3/4C	1C	1C	1-1/4C
Peel, mixed	1T	2T	1/3C	1/2C	3/4C	1C	1C	1-1/4C	1-1/2C
Potato: flakes	1/4C	1/2C	1C	1-1/3C	2C	2-1/3C	2-3/4C	3-1/3C	3-3/4C
powdered	1T	2T	1/4C	1/3C	1/2C	2/3C	3/4C	1C	1-1/4C
Prunes:									
chopped	1T	2T	1/3C	1/2C	2/3C	3/4C	1C	1-1/4C	1-1/3C
whole pitted	1T	2T	1/3C	1/2C	2/3C	3/4C	1C	1C	1-1/4C
Raisins	2T	1/4C	1/3C	1/2C	3/4C	1C	1C	1-1/3C	1-1/2C
Rice raw: long	1T	2T	1/3C	1/2C	3/4C	1C	1-1/4C	1-1/3C	1-1/2C
short grain	1T	2T	1/4C	1/2C	2/3C	3/4C	1C	1C	1-1/4C
Rice bubbles	2/3C	1-1/4C	2-1/4C	3-2/3C	5C	6-1/4C	7-1/2C	8-3/4C	10C
Rolled Oats	2T	1/3C	2/3C	1C	1-1/3C	1-3/4C	2C	2-1/2C	2-3/4C
Sago	2T	1/4C	1/3C	1/2C	3/4C	1C	1C	1-1/4C	1-1/2C
Salt	3t	6t	1/4C	1/3C	1/2C	2/3C	3/4C	1C	1C
Semolina	1T	2T	1/3C	1/2C	3/4C	1C	1C	1-1/3C	1-1/2C
Spices	6t	3T	1/4C	1/3C	1/2C	1/2C	2/3C	3/4C	1C
Sugar	3t	6t	1/4C	1/3C	1/2C	2/3C	3/4C	1C	1C
Sugar castor	3t	5t	1/4C	1/3C	1/2C	2/3C	3/4C	1C	1-1/4C
Sugar, icing	1T	2T	1/3C	1/2C	3/4C	1C	1C	1-1/4C	1-1/2C
Sugar, brown	1T	2T	1/3C	1/2C	3/4C	1C	1C	1-1/3C	1-1/2C
Sultanas	1T	2T	1/3C	1/2C	3/4C	1C	1C	1-1/4C	1-1/2C
Tapioca	1T	2T	1/3C	1/2C	2/3C	3/4C	1C	1-1/4C	1-1/3C
Treacle	2t	1T	2T	1/4C	1/3C	1/2C	1/2C	2/3C	2/3C
Walnuts:									
chopped	2T	1/4C	1/2C	3/4C	1C	1-1/4C	1-1/2C	1-3/4C	2C
halved	2T	1/3C	2/3C	1C	1-1/4C	1-1/2C	1-3/4C	2-1/4C	2-1/2C
Yeast: dried	6t	3T	1/2C	2/3C	1C	1-1/4C	1-1/3C	1-2/3C	1-3/4C
compressed	3t	6t	3T	1/3C	1/2C	1/2C	2/3C	3/4C	1C

Notes

....

....

....

....

....

....

....

....

....

....

....

....

....

....

....

....

....

....

....

....

....

....

....

....

....

The Publishers invite you to sample a taste from four of our most popular recipe books:

1. The Australian APPLE Recipe Book

APPLE ROLY POLY

2 cups S.R. flour
3 oz (90g) butter or marg.
1/3 cup butter
1 tablespoon sugar

3 apples
1/3 cup sultanas
3 tablespoons apricot jam

Sift flour, rub in butter, add water, mix to a firm dough, place on lightly floured surface, knead lightly until smooth, roll to a rectangular shape 25cm x 30cm. spread evenly with apricot jam, peel apples, grate coarsely, spread over jam, sprinkle with sultanas. Roll up starting from long side, brush joins with water. Place joined side down on greased oven tray, brush top with water, sprinkle with sugar. Bake in moderate oven 30 to 35 minutes or until golden brown. Serve with cream or custard.

SWEET CURRIED NECK CHOPS

1 large chopped onion
2 level tablespoons flour
2 level tablespoons dripping
1 level tablespoon curry powder
2 level tablespoons brown sugar
3 cups beef or chicken soup (stock)
lemon wedges and parsley to garnish

6 lamb chops
1 chopped apple
1 level teaspoon salt
juice of 1/2 lemon
seasoned flour
1/4 cup sultanas

Trim excess fat and gristle from chops. Toss in seasoned flour and fry for 15 minutes. Drain well. Prepare sauce by frying chopped apple and onion in extra dripping until lightly browned. Add flour, curry powder, brown sugar and salt, cook for 1 minute. Add stock and stir until sauce boils and thickens, then add lemon juice and sultanas. Add chops, place lid on saucepan and simmer gently for 30 minutes. Garnish with lemon wedges and parsley.

MOUTH-WATERING PUMPKIN ICE CREAM

1/2 cup cooked mashed pumpkin	1/2 teaspoon cinnamon
1/4 cup milk	1/4 teaspoon ginger
50g brown sugar	1/2 teaspoon vanilla essence
pinch salt	1 cup cream, whipped

Combine all ingredients except cream. Fold the mixture slowly into whipped cream. Pour into a shallow metal dish and freeze to the desired consistency. Makes 500ml.

PUMPKIN FRITTERS

1 beaten egg	1 teaspoon baking powder
little milk	fat or oil for frying
2 cups cooked mashed pumpkin	salt and pepper
1 cup plain flour	1/2 teaspoon dry mustard

Sift dry ingredients into bowl. Add egg and pumpkin and a little milk if too dry. Heat oil in frying pan and then drop mixture by the tablespoonful. Cook each side until brown and crisp. Drain on absorbent paper and serve at once.

PUMPKIN CAKE WITH FRUIT AND NUTS

2 teaspoons mixed spice	1-1/2 cups butter or corn oil
2 cups cooked mashed pumpkin	2 cups sugar
4 eggs, well beaten	3-1/2 cups flour
2 teaspoons vanilla	2 teaspoons baking powder
1 cup chopped nuts	2 teaspoons bicarb soda
1 cup raisins or other dried fruit	1 teaspoon salt

Cream together butter and sugar. Sift together dry ingredients, using 1 cup of the flour and add to creamed mixture along with the pumpkin. Add eggs and vanilla, beating well. Fold in nuts and raisins, which have been mixed with remaining 1/2 cup flour. Bake in a greased and floured loaf pan in a moderately hot oven for 60 minutes.

SCALLOPED POTATO PERFECTION

6 medium potatoes sliced wafer thin   Butter
Freshly ground black pepper   Salt
2 cups light cream (not a mixture)   Nutmeg

Butter a shallow baking dish no deeper than 70mm. Layer three-quarters full with potato, salt, pepper and a little nutmeg. Pour in cream just to top of potato. Dot with 2 tablespoons butter. Bake in very slow oven 120°c, 1-1/2 hours, or until potato is tender, most of cream absorbed, and top brown. Serves 6.

NOTE: Some added cheese and eggs are also good.

POTATO DUMPLINGS

8 to 10 medium potatoes   1 cup plain flour
1 egg, slightly beaten   1 teaspoon salt
Filling   Coarsely ground pepper
Chopped parsley   Melted butter or margarine
Apple or cranberry sauce

Cook potatoes until tender, drain, peel and force through sieve. Cool then add flour, egg, salt and mix until smooth. Using floured hands shape in 8cm wide roll on floured board. Cut in 10 slices, make indentation in each slice. Place 1 tablespoon filling in each, then shape in round balls to contain filling. Flatten slightly and drop in boiling salted water in large pot. slowly bring to boil and when dumplings float to surface, simmer 5 minutes. Remove to hot plate with slotted spoon, sprinkle pepper and parsley; serve with melted butter and sauce. Makes 10 dumplings.

FILLING

Mix 3 minced slices bacon, 1/2 cup chopped onion, 1/2 cup minced left over cooked meat, luncheon meat or minced meat, then saute until well browned. Drain if greasy. Season with salt and allspice.

Yorkshire Pudding

Usually served with roast beef, but is good with
all meat and poultry dishes

250g flour, sifted   2 eggs, beaten
750ml milk   Pinch salt

Place flour in basin, make well and add salt and eggs, then add milk slowly while stirring to moisten all flour. Beat well, adding remaining milk and stand 30 minutes.Grease square tin, heat until hot then pour in batter and bake 45 minutes. Serve in neatly cut squares.

Smoked Salmon Mousse

1 tablespoon gelatine   150g smoked salmon
60ml water   100ml whipped cream
2 teaspoons sugar   1 teaspoon salt
1 teaspoon dry mustard   60ml white vinegar

Sprinkle gelatine over water, add sugar, salt, mustard & vinegar. Stir over light heat until gelatine dissolves. Remove from heat and chill until nearly setting; put in salmon and blend until smooth. Fold in whipped cream, then turn into mould(s) and refrigerate. To release from mould, dip mould only in hot water for 3 seconds. Turn out on plate and serve with hot buttered brown toast.

Christmas Mince for mince pies

300g best suet   500g currants
200g candied peel   500g raisins
500g sugar   500g apples
1 tablespoon nutmeg   Peel 1 lemon, grated
10g allspice

Peel, core and finely dice apple. Mince suet, chop candied peel. Combine all ingredients mixing well; put in stone jar and press down to exclude air. Tie on cover of brown paper soaked in brandy. Leave few days before using.

Best-selling Recipe Books

from Southern Holdings

The Australian Apple Recipe Book

Includes 148 top recipes, plus orchard photographs and calendar, apple varieties, and historical apples. 8th reprint.

The Australian National Trust Recipe Book

A collection of favourite Australian family recipes, featuring the Australian National Trust Heritage in each State and Territory.

The Australian Convict Recipe Book

Includes 150 practical recipes, plus historical photographs, convict rules & rations, and the unabridged story of Bessie Baldwin.

The Great Australian Pumpkin Recipe Book

Includes 110 pumpkin recipes (including ice cream), plus the Great Pumpkin story and Growing & Caring for Pumpkins.

The Australian Potato Surprise Recipe Book

155 top potato recipes for all occasions; the versatility of this universal food is fully explored. A must for every kitchen.

The Australian Historical Recipe Book

Join John Caire in exploring Australia's most popular recipes over the years, including some introduced from Europe and Asia. Includes historical photographs and the story,"*Living Off the Land.*" Features Bush & Spade recipes, Steamboat cooking, and Homestead recipes, as well as John's own restaurant recipes.

The Australian Huon Valley Recipe Book

Authentic country recipes from the fine food centre of Tasmania. Selected from treasured family recipe collections. Beautiful Huon scenes and the settlement story are included.

The Australian Lavish Barbecue Recipe Book

An exciting approach to barbecues by a top chef - marinades, butters, breads, kebabs and Barbecues Galore combine to make this a 'must have' recipe book! Available December.

Recipe Books, per copy: $6.95 plus $1.60 P.& P.
(Fundraisers, please enquire about our special offer)
ORDER BY MAIL, PHONE OR FAX FROM:
Southern Holdings Pty Ltd P.O. Huonville 7109, Australia.
Phone: (002)664112; Fax: (002)664112. Credit card orders
accepted. All orders sent return mail by Australia Post.